IN THE KITCHEN WITH BILL

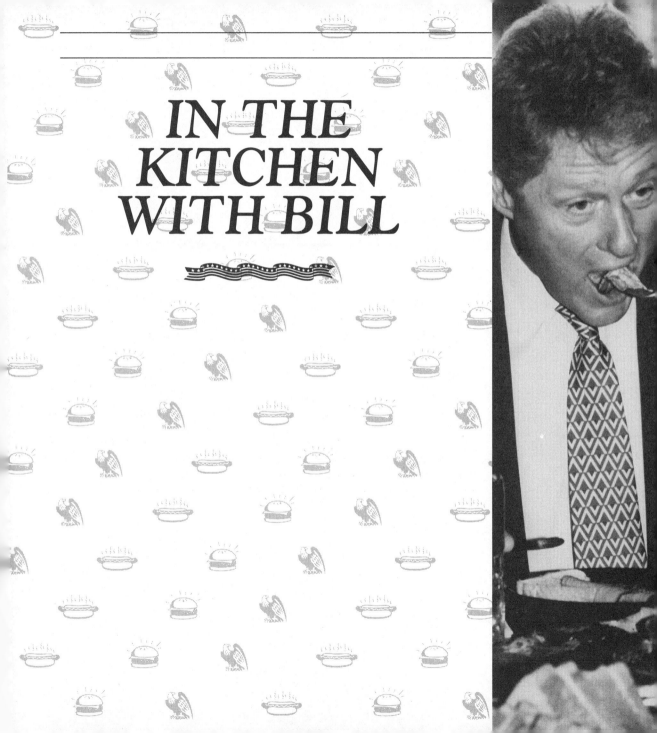

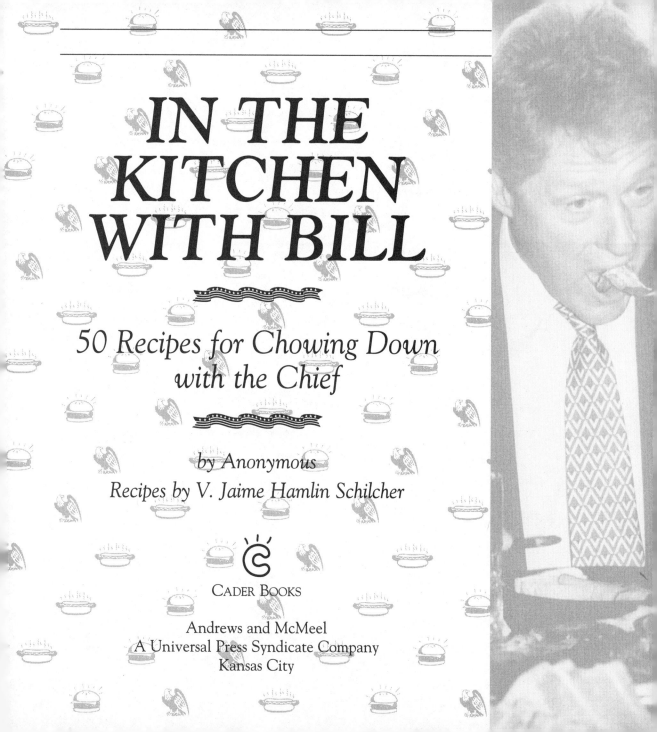

IN THE KITCHEN WITH BILL

50 Recipes for Chowing Down with the Chief

by Anonymous

Recipes by V. Jaime Hamlin Schilcher

C̆

CADER BOOKS

Andrews and McMeel
A Universal Press Syndicate Company
Kansas City

THANK YOU for buying this Cader Book—we hope you enjoy it. And thanks as well to the store that sold you this, and the hardworking sales rep who sold it to them. It takes a lot of people to make a book (even a silly one). Here are some of the many who were instrumental:

EDITORIAL: Genevieve Field, Jane Cavolina, Lisa Jenner Hudson, Jenny Bent, Jake Morrissey, Dorothy O'Brien, Regan Brown
DESIGN: Charles Kreloff, Orit Mardkha-Tenzer
RESEARCH: Cathryn Steeves
PHOTO RESEARCH: Meg Handler
COPY EDITING: Philip Reynolds
PRODUCTION: Carol Coe, Cathy Kirkland
LEGAL: Renee Schwartz, Esq.

If you would like to share any thoughts about this book, or are interested in other books by us, please write to Cader Books, 38 E. 29 Street, New York, NY, 10016.

Share your favorite recipes with the President and us on our new web site: http://www.cader-books.com

Grateful acknowledgment is made for permission to reprint the doughnut recipe from *Fit for a King*® © 1992 by Elizabeth McKeon, Ralph Gevirtz and Julie Bandy and reprinted by permission of Rutledge Hill Press, Nashville, Tennessee.

Grateful acknowledgement is also made for permission to reprint a selection from the Clinton-McDonald's sketch from *Saturday Night Live: The First 20 Years*, © 1995 Cader Company Inc., published by Houghton Mifflin Company in association with Broadway Video.

Grateful acknowledgment is also made for permission to reprint recipes on pages 25, 47, 54, and 104 from *Thirty Years at the Mansion: Recipes and Recollections* by Liza Ashley. Reprinted by permission of August House Publishers, Inc.

Library of Congress Number: 96-83763

ISBN: 0-8362-1497-8
April 1996

10 9 8 7 6 5 4 3 2 1

ATTENTION SCHOOLS AND BUSINESSES:
Andrews and McMeel books are available at quantity discounts with bulk purchase for educational, business, or sales promotional use. For information, please write to: Special Sales Department, Andrews and McMeel, 4900 Main Street, Kansas City, Missouri 64112.

"*I don't necessarily consider McDonald's junk food. You know, they have chicken sandwiches, they have salads.*"

—BILL CLINTON

CONTENTS

Photo Credits

Acknowledgments

We would also like to thank the following restaurants for donating recipes or recipe ideas in honor of Bill:

ESPRESSO LOVE for Espresso Love's Presidential Muffins;

THE OZARK MOUNTAIN FAMILY SMOKEHOUSE for 3 Things to Do with Arkansas Bacon for Breakfast;

THE NUGGET for The Nugget's 3-in-1 Burger;

GATES BAR-B-Q for Gates's Good-Time Chili;

RAGIN' CAJUN for Ragin' Cajun's Red Beans and Rice with Andouille Sausage;

PARMA PIEROGIES for Parma Pierogies;

BOMBAY CLUB for Bombay Club's Chicken Tikka Makhani;

TRIO'S for Trio's Spinach Dip with Peppery Pita Chips;

ELI'S FINEST CHEESECAKE for Eli's Caramel Praline Cheesecake.

Some recipes have been altered slightly from their original versions for cooking at home.

The White House Pantry

Our imagined look at the private presidential stash,
well stocked with all of Bill's favorite forbidden snacks.

Introduction

Coming all the way to Washington from Little Rock, Arkansas was a big adjustment for the Clinton family. Life inside the Beltway is a whole lot faster, and a whole lot meaner, and before you knew it, Bill was embroiled in controversies over everything from gays in the military to health care reform and whatever it was that happened in Whitewater. And to top it all off, there was unrest in the White House kitchen (the longtime chef was fired), and unease in the presidential stomach. Thousands of miles away from a decent barbecue joint, things started off so badly that the leader of the free world had to get up and jog all the way to McDonald's just to get himself a decent breakfast. And then to make things worse, people started saying Bill wasn't the real power in the White House—that he couldn't even pick his own menu.

But as time has proven, although he may change political positions now and then, in the kitchen with Bill there's no lack of resolution. Like the country he leads, Clinton is a man with big appetites. So it's only natural that sometimes, like the government itself, his desires don't necessarily fit his caloric budget. But we Americans like to have it all, and Clinton's position on the dishes of the day puts him squarely of the people, by the people, and for the people. In a time when rampant political correctness is curbing the rights of average Americans to think, say, and, more impor-

SOME OF BILL'S FAVORITE FOODS:

Sliced pork barbecue
Baked beans
Sweet potatoes
Soft tacos
Enchiladas
Cream pies
Cinnamon rolls
Banana anything
Mango ice cream
Dunkin' Donuts
Bojangle's biscuits
Jell-O salad
McDonald's Egg
McMuffins
Domino's pizza

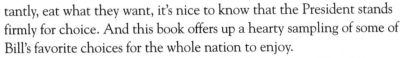

tantly, eat what they want, it's nice to know that the President stands firmly for choice. And this book offers up a hearty sampling of some of Bill's favorite choices for the whole nation to enjoy.

Whatever may come in the days ahead, one part of the Clinton legacy is already barbecued into the history books—we all feel a little freer now to chow down, and we have Bill to thank for that. When it comes to eating, he takes the cake.

How Presidential Is It?

A symbol appears at the end of every recipe indicating its relative calorie content, with particular emphasis on its overall fattiness. Until you can eat a five-elephant dish without guilt, take 12 steps to the nearest bag of nachos and force yourself. You'll feel better for it.

Congressional
(100–200 calories per serving)

Senatorial
(200–400 calories per serving)

Cabinet level
(400–600 calories per serving)

🐘 🐘 🐘 🐘

Presidential nominee. Do you have what it takes to go oval?
(600–700 calories per serving)

🐘 🐘 🐘 🐘 🐘

The buck stops here—you've busted the budget and claimed the top prize.
(700+ calories per serving)

All recipes serve four unless otherwise noted.

IN THE KITCHEN WITH BILL

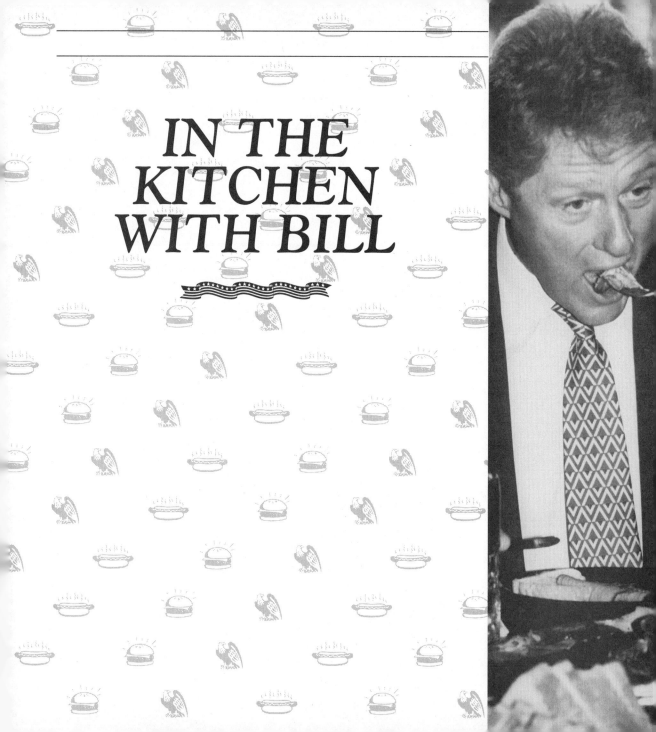

Breakfast of Champions

Washington is all about secrets—anything important usually gets leaked and the most mundane details are tightly protected. To that end, the White House press office apparently regards the President's breakfast menu as privileged information. For the record, the official position on Bill's first binge of the day is: "Regarding the President's breakfast, I can't get a straight answer for you. But I can tell you he tries to eat a healthy, well-balanced breakfast every day and would encourage kids to do the same."

We do know that when our man Bill was on his way to victory in the New Hampshire primary, he fueled himself with a very special breakfast. Actually he ate breakfast all day long, haunting the Dunkin' Donuts (as vividly portrayed in *Primary Colors*). So peruse the following and select your own Breakfast of Champions.

ESPRESSO LOVE'S PRESIDENTIAL MUFFINS

When Carol McManus, proprietor and baker at Espresso Love, a bakery in Edgartown on Martha's Vineyard, learned of the President's impending visit in 1993, she was so excited that she invented a new recipe to tempt Bill's appetite. Her Presidential Muffin contained a patriotic collection of strawberries, cream cheese and blueberries. It was a big hit with customers, but sadly, Bill never came by for a taste.

A year passed, and Carol's Presidential Muffins became Espresso Love's hottest-selling item—second place went to the First Lady Muffin, a healthier treat made with apples and oatmeal—but still no Bill. Then, in the summer of 1994, when the Clintons returned to Martha's Vineyard, a presidential aide walked into Espresso Love's and ordered two Presidential Muffins, two First Lady Muffins, and bagels and scones, all for the First Family. (A separate order was made for the White House staff.) This became the standard order during the rest of the Clintons' vacation. After a number of such breakfasts, Bill finally came by for an early morning visit, "To meet the lady who does the baking."

Makes 18–20 muffins.

2¾ cups all-purpose flour
¾ cup plus 2 tablespoons sugar
1 tablespoon baking powder
1 teaspoon salt
½ cup (1 stick) butter, melted
8 ounces cream cheese, softened

¾ cup milk
1 teaspoon vanilla extract
2 eggs
¾ cup blueberries
½ cup strawberries, chopped

Preheat oven to 375 degrees. Stir together flour, sugar, baking powder and salt.

In a food processor combine melted butter, cream cheese, milk, vanilla and eggs until smooth. Pour into dry ingredients and stir quickly until just combined. Stir in fruit. *Do not overmix.*

Spray muffin tins with nonstick spray. Fill ¾ full. Sprinkle tops with sugar.

Bake approximately 15 minutes or until muffins spring back when pressed.

FAT CONTENT RATING:

"Early rising is also essential to the good government of a family. A late breakfast deranges the whole business of the day and throws a portion of it on the next, which opens the door for confusion to enter."

–MARTHA JEFFERSON RANDOLPH, daughter of Thomas Jefferson, in her cookbook, *The Virginia Housewife* (1824)

DONUTS FIT FOR THE KING

The truth is somewhat shocking: Elvis Presley, whose favorite foods mostly mirrored those of his biggest fan, Bill Clinton, didn't like donuts. Yet, like Bill (who has oft been spotted munching on Dunkin' Donuts), the King was frequently parodied as a sort of Donut Dervish. The rumors about Presley got started back when the King was just a bedroom-eyed boy-next-door, singing occasional gigs at the Louisiana Hayride in Memphis. At that time, he sang his first and only radio commercial, for Southern Maid Donuts—a gig that earned him VIP status with donut lovers nationwide.

3 tablespoons vegetable shortening
⅔ cup sugar
2 eggs, well beaten
3½ cups sifted all-purpose flour
4 teaspoons baking powder
½ teaspoon salt
⅔ cup milk
Confectioners' sugar

In a mixing bowl cream the shortening with the sugar. Add the eggs and blend. In a separate bowl sift together the flour, baking powder and salt and add them to the creamed mixture alternately with the milk. Turn the dough onto a floured board and roll to 1-inch thickness. Cut with floured donut cutter.

Fry the donuts a few at a time in deep hot fat (365 degrees). Turn just as soon as the donuts rise to the top. Turn once or twice during the frying process. Drain on paper towels. Let the donuts cool. Dust with confectioners' sugar.

FAT CONTENT RATING:

HUBCAP CINNAMON ROLLS

Bill likes his cinnamon rolls "big as hubcaps," according to Ann Ward of Hungry's Café, where the former Arkansas governor used to stop some mornings for a family-sized cinnamon bun. Of course the calorie-conscious Clinton would smear his oversized sticky rolls with margarine instead of butter, so it wasn't really as indulgent as it seems. Perhaps not entirely by coincidence, Hungry's closed down shortly after the Clintons left the Governor's Mansion for the White House.

½ cup (1 stick) butter
1¾ cup sugar
1 teaspoon salt
⅔ cup milk
2 packs active yeast
½ cup warm water
6 cups all-purpose flour
2 eggs
¼ cup melted butter
1 tablespoon cinnamon
¼ cup raisins
1 cup pecans, chopped then toasted

In a pan melt butter. Add ¾ cup of the sugar, salt and milk. Heat and stir until butter is melted.

Dissolve yeast in a large mixing bowl by adding warm water. Make sure to follow dissolving tips on packet of yeast. Mix in butter mixture.

Using an electric mixer blend in 3 cups of the flour and one egg

THE BUSHELL BREAKFAST

George Bush was known for doing a lot of things more quickly than most of us: playing golf, driving his boat and eating. In fact he often ate like a teenager, gobbling down nachos, steaks or egg rolls with equal gusto. It follows suit that Bush should take the prize for the most unpresidential breakfast in presidential history: oatmeal with a Butterfinger bar crumbled on top.

yolk, making sure to save the white for glazing.

Finally mix in the rest of the flour (2–3 cups, enough to make a small ball).

Knead the dough on a floured board until uniformly smooth (10 to 20 minutes). Use flour to prevent the dough from sticking.

Place dough in a greased bowl. Turn over so exposed top is greased. Cover and let rise for 2 hours in a warm place.

Put dough on floured board; knead to release air. Roll dough out to a thin rectangle (18x24 inches). Cover rolled dough with ¼ cup melted butter. Sprinkle 1 cup sugar mixed with cinnamon. Sprinkle raisins and pecans. Roll up dough; cut into 6 equal rolls. Brush surface with egg whites and 1 teaspoon water. Place in greased glass pan. Cook at preheated 350-degree oven for 35 minutes.

FAT CONTENT RATING:

EASY EGG MCCLINTONS

In his early days in office, Bill was known to lead his famous morning jogs past the McDonald's on 17th Street, taking a brief "energy break" for an Egg McMuffin. These public jogs were brought to a quick end—some say it was for security reasons, others say it was for dietary reasons (and others still maintain it was to protect the public from the presidential thighs)—and a jogging track was installed on White House grounds. But whipping up your own post-jogging treat is pretty easy. Our fat-reduced presidential version leaves out the mayonnaise.

2 tablespoons butter or margarine
4 eggs
4 English muffins
4 slices of ham
4 slices American cheese

Fry eggs in butter or margarine until done to desired standard.

Toast muffins, place eggs on bottom half of muffin, layer ham then American cheese on top of egg.

Broil until cheese is melted.

Top with other half of muffin and enjoy.

FAT CONTENT RATING: 🐘 🐘 🐘

"That he didn't inhale [marijuana] becomes unbelievable to anyone who's seen him eat at a McDonald's."

–DEE DEE MYERS

CLINTON DOES McDONALD'S

Soon after his election, *Saturday Night Live* presented Clinton at his McDonald's-munching best. Here is an excerpt from that now-classic sketch.

Clinton [Enters, wearing Arkansas Razorbacks sweatshirt and mini jogging shorts]:...You got a real American family place here. Is it too late for an Egg McMuffin?

McD's Manager: Well, we stop serving breakfast at eleven. But for you ...

Clinton: Thanks so much.

McD's Manager: And should I check to see if I can scare up some of those sausage patties?

Clinton: You read my mind.

Aide [whispers]: Ah, sir, maybe you'd prefer a McLean Burger, or the garden salad is very nice.

College-Aged Customer: Governor Clinton. Ah, I'm a sophomore in college, and I may have to drop out because my parents can't afford tuition.

Clinton: Speak of the devil, that's one of those McLean sandwiches. Are those any good?

College-Aged Customer: Would you like to try it?

Clinton: Well, just a bite. Mmm. That's not bad. You know, my National Service Trust Fund would allow every student to—Mind if I wash it down? Ah! That hits the spot.

McD's Manager: Your Egg McMuffin, Mr. President.

Clinton: Thank you, Kevin. You have any of that sweet and sour sauce? You know, the kind that you dip McNuggets in.

McD's Manager: For your McMuffin?

Clinton: Or the barbecue sauce. Whichever.

Other Customer: You can use mine.

Clinton: Great. Just pour it right on.

Other Customer: I have a question.

Clinton: That's it. Pour it all on.

Other Customer: Do you support the decision to send troops to Somalia?

Clinton [Taking a bite]: Mmm, that's a good question. Yes, I do, and let me tell you why. See, right now, we're sending in *[Holds up his McMuffin]*…food *[Puts McMuffin in front of other customer]*…to Somalia …but it's not getting to the people who need it…because *[Brings McMuffin back to himself]*…it's being intercepted by the warlords. *[Finishes McMuffin]* And it's not just us. It's other countries too.

[Grabs a McNugget from yet another customer] Your McNugget is aid from Great Britain. *[Starts to take it to previous customer, but then gobbles it down.]* Intercepted by warlords. *[Looks around; finds…]* This man's Filet-O-Fish over here is relief from Italy. *[Pops it in his mouth; a muffled…]* Warlords. And you can send all the food you want. *[Grabbing…]* A McDLT, hot apple pie, it's just gonna end up with *[Eating]*…the warlords. Now, with a broad-based international military force, we can make sure that the…McRib Sandwich…*[Grabs a McRib and sets it on other customer's tray]*…gets to the people who need it. *[Then he just picks it up and gulps it down.]* Can I get a Coke?

3 THINGS TO DO WITH ARKANSAS BACON FOR BREAKFAST

L est anyone think that government does not concern itself with the serious issues, the Arkansas legislature stood tall in their passage of Act 326, which regulates local bacon. As a result, the prized appellation "Arkansas Bacon" can only be worn by bacon that meets specific qualifications. It must come from "high on the hog," above the shoulder and in front of the loin, where there's more lean meat. This rare meat must be cured the old-fashioned way, hand-rubbed with dry sugar cure. Water may not be added. Finally, Arkansas Bacon is slowly smoked with hickory wood instead of imitation liquid smoke.

The Ozark Mountain Family Smokehouse is the President's preferred supplier, and more than a thousand slices were ordered for Clinton preinauguration events. The Family Smokehouse provided these recipes from their *Ozark Mountain Cookbook*. If you absolutely can't get your mitts on Arkansas Bacon, it's okay to use regular bacon.

QUICK SUNDAY BRUNCH

Toast a split English muffin and place a layer of cooked Arkansas Bacon on each half. Place a poached egg on the bacon and cover with any brand of cheese sauce.

FAT CONTENT RATING:

EGGS BENEDICT

Place one or two slices of Arkansas Bacon on top of a toasted English muffin. Place a poached egg on top of meat and cover with Hollandaise sauce.

QUICK HOLLANDAISE SAUCE

Place yolks from 3 eggs, juice from a lemon, a teaspoon salt and a teaspoon black pepper in a blender and mix well. While blender is on, slowly add a cup of melted butter. Serve immediately or keep warm in the top of a double boiler over hot water.

FAT CONTENT RATING:

BATTERED AND FRIED BACON WITH CREAM GRAVY

Dip bacon strips in flour and fry in pan with ½ inch bacon fat. Pour off all but 2 tablespoons of fat, add same amount of flour. Cook and stir until flour is browned. Add 1 to 2 cups milk gradually, stirring constantly to prevent lumps. Salt and pepper to taste. When gravy boils up and thickens, serve over biscuits or grits.

FAT CONTENT RATING: 🐘 🐘 🐘 🐘 🐘

> *"It turns out that back in 1980, Hillary Clinton invested in sugar, hogs and cattle. She got the idea from watching her husband eat breakfast."*
>
> –CONAN O'BRIEN

WARREN WAFFLES, TOO

There's been talk of waffles in the White House long before Bill Clinton came along. Indeed, President Harding was a particularly unorthodox waffle eater, and preferred to top his discs with creamed chipped beef. Try it for dinner. For a lighter early morning meal, serve these with butter, maple syrup, honey or jam. This recipe comes from the Harding-era *Stag Cook Book: Written for Men by Men*, collected and edited by C. Mac Sheridan (1922).

2 eggs, separated
2 tablespoons sugar
1 teaspoon salt
2 tablespoons butter
1 pint milk
Flour as needed to make thin batter
2 large teaspoons baking powder

Beat yolks of eggs, add sugar and salt. Melt butter and add to mixture, along with milk and flour. Just before you are ready to bake, add stiffly beaten whites of eggs and baking powder.
    Bake in a hot, lightly oiled waffle iron.

FAT CONTENT RATING:

Flip-Flopping
(Burgers, That Is)

Bill has been accused of occasionally changing his views on the passing issues of the day, like gays in the military, health care, Medicare, Bosnia, Somalia and other areas of concern, but let's cut him a break. Like any good maître d', he knows you have to change the menu frequently to keep the patrons happy. And isn't it only right that a president who was elected by far less than half the electorate should be comfortable with more than one side of an issue? Flip! Traditional Democrats get their agenda aired. Flop! Moderate independents get equal time from their president, too. Like grilling a good hamburger, the whole thing is better done after a couple of flips.

But burgers are one issue on which we all come together. And here the President stands solidly with the people—flip 'em, flop 'em, those patties will also fly.

THE NUGGET'S 3-IN-1 BURGER

This president is not just an eater, he's an inventor. When visiting the Nugget in Summerland, California, in December 1992 in the heady transition days, Clinton brought his bold style and fresh new ideas to the menu. The accomplishment was a classic Clinton maneuver, bringing opposing sides to the table and banging out a compromise.

In this particular case, the problem was a hole in the burger selection. Bill brought together three different Nugget sandwiches in his very own Rainbow Burger. Who else would have the vision to unite a quarter-pound sourdough cheeseburger (minus the cheese) with Ortega chilies from another burger and hickory-flavored "Hick" Sauce from an altogether third burger?

Having just come from a barbecue in their honor, Bill and Hillary modestly split the burger and found just enough room to do the same with a generous portion of Nugget Nachos.

An inspiration to diplomacy of all kinds, here is our slightly modified version of the now-famous Nugget Burger.

1¼ pounds ground beef
2 tablespoons minced onion
Salt and pepper to taste
¼ cup hot water
4 slices Cheddar cheese
¼ cup sliced green chilies
Arkansas "Hick" Sauce (recipe follows)

In a large bowl combine the beef, onion, salt and pepper.

Measure out the meat in ⅓ cup portions and shape into patties about ½ inch thick.

Sprinkle ¼ teaspoon of salt in the bottom of a heavy skillet. Brown both sides of the patties.

Cover and reduce the heat. Top with cheese. Cook to desired doneness. Remove the hamburgers and add the hot water to the skillet.

Blend in a serving of Arkansas "Hick" Sauce and slices of hot chili peppers to make pan gravy.

Pour the gravy over patties, serve on toasted rolls.

FAT CONTENT RATING: 🐘 🐘 🐘 🐘

ARKANSAS "HICK" SAUCE

Here's our version of the Nugget's "Hick" Sauce.

2 tablespoons butter
1 small onion, chopped
3 cloves garlic, crushed
½ cup cider vinegar
½ cup brown sugar
2 bay leaves
½ teaspoon hot chili powder
½ teaspoon salt

Melt butter in small saucepan and sauté onion and garlic until softened. Add the rest of the ingredients and simmer on low heat 10 minutes. Remove bay leaves and serve with the Nugget's 3-in-1 Burger (see recipe).

THE BIGGEST BILL

Clinton may be a bit portly, but he can't hold a candle to the most overweight president in history, William Howard Taft, who weighed in at 350 pounds. His girth necessitated the installation of a special bathtub in the White House. Teddy Roosevelt once advised Taft, known as "Big Bill," to forgo horseback riding as it would be "dangerous for him and cruelty to the horse." On a similar note, while serving as governor-general of the Philippines, Taft cabled this message to Secretary of War Elihu Root: "Took long horseback ride today; feeling fine." Root responded, "How is the horse?"

CAMPAIGN
STYLES
OF THE
HUNGRY
AND
FAMOUS

Does Bill have the stamina to go the distance? On the campaign trail in 1992, Clinton assured himself of the beef industry's support by stopping to sample the goods at as many as eight diners and barbecues a day. Impressive, but far from record-setting: Ulysses S. Grant didn't travel much to gather his food, but he was known to feast on a steady stream of as many as 29 courses.

WHITEWATER WAFFLE BURGER

This one's for Hillary, because, after all is said and done, we still admire her. Who else with a vocabulary of June Cleaver-esque phrases like "What's up, buttercup?" and "Okey-dokey, artichokey" could turn a $1,000 investment into $100,000? Does anyone outside of Washington really care about (or understand) her lost investment in some Arkansas pasture? What other First Lady could go head to head with a grand jury and come sailing through the rapids? Hillary can take the heat, so she surely can take the heat of this commemorative waffle.

2 pounds ground beef
2 tablespoons taco seasoning
4 hamburger buns
Sliced jalapeño peppers to taste
4 slices raw onion
4 slices Monterey Jack cheese
Salt and pepper
Ranch dressing

Preheat waffle iron. In a large bowl, add taco seasoning to ground beef, mix well, and form burgers. When iron is hot, put in burgers and cook approximately 3 minutes per side or until almost done. Toast buns separately. Top burgers with sliced jalapeños, onions and cheese, put into burger rolls, return entire assembly to waffle iron. Push down hard on lid, cook for about 2 minutes or until cheese is melted.

Serve with lots of ranch dressing.

FAT CONTENT RATING:

A LITTLE CHAMPAGNE WITH HIS CAKE

Mrs. Grant was, like Mrs. Clinton, often concerned over her husband's public image. While Hillary keeps her eye on Bill's girth (and his occasionally wandering eye), Julia worried about Ulysses's drinking. As an afterthought, and, we assume, in a slight bow to his wife, the 18th president requested that she send up cake with the bubbly, though, we also assume, he had no intention of eating it.

GATES'S GOOD-TIME CHILI

Down home in Arkansas, barbecue is pretty straight-forward, but in Kansas City, there's a serious rivalry between Gates Bar-B-Q and Ricky's. Proprietor Ricky Smith, who actually hails from Arkansas, supplied food for the President's inauguration and fueled him on the campaign trail back in 1992. Ricky also supplied ribs, sausage and beans for Clinton's subsequent town hall meeting on health care. In a backfired attempt at being politic, Clinton operatives had actually led both Ricky's and Gates to believe that they were the official caterers for the event. But it turned out Gates just got to feed the media and others.

Never one to alienate any segment of the body gastronomic, Bill made up for the slight later that year. "Finally, a president comes around to Gates," crowed owner Ollie Gates, who served up what was then called a Mixed Tray (since rechristened the "President's Choice Tray"), consisting of barbecued ribs, beef, chicken, bread and french fries.

1 pound ground beef
1 16-ounce can diced or whole peeled tomatoes, undrained
1 15-ounce can red kidney beans, drained and rinsed
½ cup Gates Original Classic Sauce*
1 small onion, sliced
1 green pepper, sliced
1 cup Cheddar cheese, shredded

Seasonings to taste:
Salt
Pepper
Garlic salt
Chili seasoning

In a large skillet, brown ground beef. Drain fat. Season to taste. Stir in diced or whole peeled tomatoes and red kidney beans. Bring to a boil, stirring frequently. Reduce heat; cover and simmer 5 minutes. Add barbecue sauce and simmer an additional 5 minutes. Garnish with onions, green peppers and cheese.

FAT CONTENT RATING: 🐘 🐘 🐘 🐘

*See Mail-Order Sources (page 114) to order, or substitute your favorite barbecue sauce.

Apparently Haller did "learn" to use the proper cut of chuck, since his tenure at the White House lasted through the Reagan years, though in his own White House Family Cookbook, his chili recipe still allowed for "2 pounds lean ground chuck or round steak."

BILL'S KITCHEN HINTS

Though Clinton's usual role in the kitchen is as a consumer, he does have a few cooking secrets up his sleeve. Apparently, one Thanksgiving the staff at the Governor's Mansion cooked a turkey ahead of time and left instructions to reheat it before dinner. But to some people a holiday without pork is like a day without sunshine, so Clinton decided to liven things up with a few bacon strips. He couldn't find toothpicks to attach the meat, so he used yellow corn-holders shaped like tiny ears of corn. An hour later, the turkey was basted with a veneer of melted yellow plastic.

SLOPPY STATE OF THE UNION JOES

Slopping on the political platitudes, at the last State of the Union message, Bill told everyone what they wanted to hear, but little about the state of the union. While many viewers weren't sure what they'd learned from the President's election-year address, most of us at least felt a tinge patriotic and nodded our heads in agreement with Bill's promises to "Leave our environment safe and clean for the next generation," "Cherish our children and strengthen America's family," "Take our streets back from crime and gangs and drugs" and "Maintain America's leadership in the fight for freedom and peace." Heck, if nothing else, the President reminded the American people of our fondness for the things this country was founded on: Life, Liberty, Apple Pie and Sloppy Joes.

1½ pounds ground beef
1 small onion, chopped
2 cloves garlic, minced
1 green pepper, chopped
6 ounces tomato paste
1½ cups water
1 package Sloppy Joe seasoning

Brown beef in large skillet, remove from pan, drain and set aside. Sauté the onion, garlic and green pepper in drippings. Add tomato paste, water and Sloppy Joe seasoning. Place on toasted hamburger buns.

FAT CONTENT RATING:

THE WHITE HOUSE
WASHINGTON

PRESIDENT EISENHOWER'S RECIPE
FOR OLD-FASHIONED BEEF STEW

(For six portions)

2 lbs. stewing beef (Prime round)

1 lb. small Irish potatoes

1 bunch small carrots

3/4 lb. small onions

2 fresh tomatoes

Assorted spices (thyme, bay leaves, garlic, etc.)
in cloth bag.

2-1/2 pints beef stock

Salt

Pepper

Accent

Stew meat until tender, add vegetables and spices. Cook until vegetables are done, strain off one cup of stock from stew, thicken slightly with beef roux mixture. Pour back into stew and let simmer until ready to serve (about one-half hour).

Although Eisenhower's heart attack in 1955 slowed him down, he wasn't averse to some good old-fashioned American cooking, and had his own favorite beef stew recipe.

A RARE BREED

Reagan was one of the few presidents who didn't take his steak medium rare. He liked it well done. The Gipper also liked hamburger soup made with ground beef, tomatoes and carrots. Other favorites were roast beef hash and beef and kidney pie. Mrs. Reagan was considered a "picky eater" by the White House staff. Both Reagans enjoyed such desserts as apple brown Betty, prune whip, fruit with Cointreau and plum pudding.

WILD BILL BUFFALO BURGERS

Due in large part to private farmers raising this country's "first natural cattle" as livestock, the American Bison, known in the 1800s as "The Lord of the Plains," has returned in record numbers and is no longer considered an endangered species. This is a burger that Bill can enjoy relatively guilt free because the unique characteristics of the buffalo do not allow it to become "marbled" with fat. The Denver Buffalo Company sums up the appeal of bison meat best, saying, "Buffalo tastes like beef wishes it did."

2 pounds buffalo burger
4 hamburger buns
½ cup mayonnaise
3 scallions, chopped
Salt and pepper to taste

FOR THE SAUCE/MARINADE:
¼ cup brown sugar
½ cup soy sauce
½ cup pineapple juice
1 tablespoon ground ginger root
2 large cloves minced garlic
1 tablespoon sesame oil
¼ teaspoon oil

In medium bowl combine sauce ingredients; stir together thoroughly.

Form burgers. Marinate burgers in sauce while you make the scallion mayonnaise. Combine chopped scallions and mayonnaise in food processor, blend about 30 seconds.

Heat vegetable oil in a large skillet on high, remove burgers from marinade, pat dry. Cook burgers in skillet approximately 3 minutes per side until desired doneness. (Buffalo meat cooks fast. Don't leave patties on the grill too long or meat will toughen.)

Bring sauce/marinade to a boil in a small saucepan. Reduce by one-third and serve on the side of the buffalo burgers. Toast rolls, spread with scallion mayonnaise.

FAT CONTENT RATING:

Chin-Up Chicken Fried Steak

This classic dish is particularly popular at truck stops and diners across the southern states, where truckers and road-trippers stop at all hours for a good honest pick-me-up. We've heard Bill likes to do all kinds of things in his pickup truck, and can only imagine that one of those things includes eating.

½ bottle of beer
2 egg yolks
1 tablespoon melted butter
½ teaspoon Tabasco sauce
2 teaspoons soy sauce
1 teaspoon garlic powder
1⅔ cups all-purpose flour
4 thick 16-ounce sirloins
1 cup vegetable oil
sliced white bread
2 cups canned chicken gravy

In a small bowl mix beer, egg yolks, melted butter, Tabasco and soy sauce. In a large bowl, add beer-egg mixture to garlic powder and 1⅓ cups of the flour and mix well. Let batter sit 3 hours.

Cut sirloins in half crosswise. Pound until thin and tenderized.

Dredge the four steaks in the remaining ⅓ cup flour.

Heat oil in large skillet. Batter steaks and fry on both sides 3 to 5 minutes.

Serve on toasted white bread and smother with heated chicken gravy.

FAT CONTENT RATING:

SLICK WILLIE'S WISHBONE TENDERS

BILL ATE HERE
BILL ATE HERE

The presidency naturally involves a lot of entertaining. When guests come calling, there's nothing that Bill hankers for more than some beef soaked in bottled dressing. During Clinton's days as governor of Arkansas, chef Liza Ashley had orders to start up this specialty whenever guests came by the Governor's Mansion. Try it out the next time you feel like entertaining presidentially.

6 pounds beef tenders
1 16-ounce bottle Wishbone Italian salad dressing
Coarse-ground black pepper to taste

Marinate meat in salad dressing for 4 to 5 hours, turning periodically.
    Sprinkle with pepper.
    Grill on barbecue to desired doneness. This will melt in your mouth.

FAT CONTENT RATING: 🐘 🐘 🐘

"They didn't even eat squirrel like the rest of the governors, they didn't like wild things—no venison, but maybe some quail."
    –LIZA ASHLEY
Apparently raccoon didn't count as a "wild thing," since Governor Clinton always ate his share at the annual Gillett Coon Supper in southeastern Arkansas.

The Pork Barrel

Every elected official comes to Washington wanting to cut some pork—somebody else's, that is. A good look at Mr. Speaker makes it pretty clear that even the most strong-willed us of all still crave those tasty bits once in a while. No matter what the Contract with America says, the social contract puts particular emphasis on the pursuit of happiness. Pork may not belong in the budget, but it works very nicely on your plate, dripping in barbecue sauce.

SOUTHERN-STYLE BARBECUED PORK RIBS

This recipe was created in honor of Vice President Al Gore, who isn't so politically correct that he can't enjoy "the other white meat" now and then, and who can be counted on to keep a bet. The former governor of Tennessee has an ongoing rivalry with the former gov' of Arkansas over the annual pigskin battle between the universities of Arkansas and Tennessee. It led to a bet between Bill and Al: If the 18th-ranked Razorbacks were to lose at home, Clinton would have to buy Gore a steak and tamales from Doe's Eat Place in Little Rock. Should Gore's tenth-ranked Volunteers lose the game, he'd owe the President a $10.95 "large serving" of dry-cooked pork ribs from Memphis's Rendez Vous Barbecue.

As it turned out, Bill was the loser, but Al, knowing how much his boss loves barbecue, got the ribs for him anyway while visiting Memphis for a speech. They were inspected by the Secret Service and transported to the President on Air Force Two.

3 pounds pork spare ribs
2 tablespoons pickling spice
1 tablespoon salt

FOR THE BARBECUE SAUCE
2 tablespoons butter
2 cloves minced garlic
¼ cup ketchup
1 teaspoon horseradish
1 tablespoon Worcestershire sauce
1 tablespoon molasses
2 tablespoons hot sauce

1 tablespoon soy sauce
½ teaspoon crushed red pepper

In a large pot cover ribs with water, add pickling spice and salt and bring to a boil. Lower heat and simmer, covered, for approximately 1 hour. This will tenderize the ribs.

FOR THE SAUCE
In a small pan melt the butter and sauté the garlic. Remove from heat and put in a bowl. Add the rest of the ingredients, stir together thoroughly.

Remove ribs from water and pat dry. Paint with sauce and grill (or broil), turning frequently for approximately 15 minutes. Baste frequently with remaining sauce.

FAT CONTENT RATING: 🐘 🐘 🐘 🐘

PENTAGON STUFFED PORK CHOPS

The federal government is full of pork, and some say a lot of it can be found in the Pentagon. With three times the floor space of the Empire State Building, the Capitol could fit into any one of the Pentagon's five wedge-shaped sections. About 23,000 employees work there, and the food services staff of 230 oversees a dining room, two cafeterias, and six indoor and one outdoor snack bars. With all those places to eat, there ought to be at least some delicious pork to be found, like these hearty chops.

3 pounds or 4 large double-thick pork chops
4 cloves garlic
4 bay leaves, crumbled
½ teaspoon thyme leaves
1 tablespoon kosher salt
¼ teaspoon pepper
14 ounces fresh mushrooms
2 small onions
2 tablespoons olive oil
½ cup cream cheese

FOR THE SAUCE:
½ cup canned chicken broth
½ cup heavy cream
½ cup beer
1 tablespoon Worcestershire sauce
1 tablespoon Dijon mustard

Butterfly (slice halfway through) the pork chops. Mince 2 cloves of the garlic, mix with crumbled bay leaves, thyme, salt and pepper.

Coat pork chops with above mixture; let sit while you make the stuffing.

Roughly chop the mushrooms, chop the onions, mince the remaining 2 cloves garlic. Pour the olive oil into a sauté pan, adding chopped mushrooms, garlic, onion. Sauté until tender.

Remove sautéed ingredients from pan. Reserve 1 cup for sauce and stuff chops with the rest, adding in the cream cheese.

Preheat broiler, broil chops 10 minutes per side.

Take reserved mushroom and onion mixture, put it in sauce pan; sauté 1 to 2 minutes, add canned chicken broth, heavy cream, and beer (Bill likes Moosehead).

Reduce mixture over high heat by half, add Worcestershire sauce and Dijon mustard, salt and pepper to taste.

Pour over broiled chops.

FAT CONTENT RATING: 🐘 🐘 🐘 🐘 🐘

> *"There is no such thing as a healthy Southern recipe—you use the real ingredients or you don't cook Southern."*
>
> —SARA SHARP, owner, the Ozark Mountain Family Smokehouse, Fayetteville, Arkansas

RAGIN' CAJUN'S RED BEANS AND RICE WITH ANDOUILLE SAUSAGE

Danny Delcambre, chef and owner of Delcambre's Ragin' Cajun in Seattle, Washington, served this dish to Bill, who stopped by the restaurant to pay his respects to Danny and his staff, who are all deaf. This dish is a traditional Cajun meal usually served on Mondays (wash day). Although many people think Cajun cooking means hot it really means full of spice and flavor. The President likes his extra spicy, so Danny plans to give him an extra bottle of Tabasco the next time he's in town. This recipe will serve eight.

1 pound red kidney beans
1 large onion, chopped
4 cloves garlic, crushed
1 bunch scallions, chopped
4 tablespoons vegetable oil
1 green pepper, chopped
3 bay leaves
¼ teaspoon thyme
2 tablespoons parsley

1½ teaspoons cayenne pepper
1 pound tasso (Cajun ham)*
1 pound andouille sausage, sliced**
1 tablespoon salt
8 cups cooked rice

Wash beans and soak overnight in 2 quarts of water.

The next day, drain and rinse beans and bring to a boil in a large pot in 2 quarts of water. Simmer gently for one hour.

Sauté onion, garlic and scallions in vegetable oil until translucent. Add green pepper and sauté for 3 minutes more. Add this, plus all other ingredients (except rice) to the pot and simmer for another hour, stirring occasionally.

To serve, ladle over the cooked white rice.

FAT CONTENT RATING:

*Tasso is a spicy Cajun ham. If you can't find it, substitute a baked ham slice cut into 1-inch cubes and increase the cayenne pepper, adjusting to taste.

**Andouille sausage is a very spicy Cajun sausage. Italian sausage can be substituted here.

PANETTA'S PIGS IN A BLANKET

Bill's chief of staff is a hardworking son of Italian immigrants who has called his position "the toughest job in Washington." Leon Panetta has to wrap a comforting cloak around all kinds of things that come the President's way, and here's the perfect dish to go with the task.

4 all-beef hot dogs
2 cups leftover chili
4 tortillas
½ cup smooth-melt cheese (about 2 tablespoons per serving)

Boil hot dogs in water. Reheat chili.

Warm tortillas in 200-degree oven. Take out tortillas and place on serving plates. Spread each with about ½ cup of chili and 2 tablespoons smooth-melt cheese. Place a hot dog in the center of each and wrap up. Serve with plenty of antacids.

FAT CONTENT RATING: 🐘 🐘 🐘 🐘

French Fried Nation

"I don't necessarily consider McDonald's junk food. You know, they have chicken sandwiches, they have salads," said the President.

And, let's face it, they also have fries, which exert more of a pull on Bill and the rest of us than rabbit food ever could. You don't jog all the way to McDonald's for a salad.

Why our love affair with things fried? Why are we compelled to munch on things that have been sizzling in hot oil?

Perhaps our national attachment to french fries is a lasting expression of our gratitude to Lafayette. But everything—onion rings, potatoes, fish, even plain old dough—is just, well, better, cooked that way. Take these crunchy, dripping delights away from most Americans and there'll be a real oil crisis to contend with.

"Give me a break—I mean, you're talking about a guy who jogs through McDonald's. I'm sure he'd try anything, but when it comes down to it, he seems to love the richer stuff the best."

—RANDY BATES of Trio's, one of Bill's favorite Little Rock hangouts

CHELSEA'S SPICY CURLY FRIES

The curly-haired Clinton kid, like most kids, likes french fries. Other Chelsea favorites include hamburgers, macaroni and cheese (a passion she shares with President Reagan), chicken pot pie, grilled cheese sandwiches and carrot cake (see Chelsea's Birthday Carrot Cake, page 92).

1 bag Ore-Ida frozen curly fries
¼ teaspoon Cajun seasoning
Salt and pepper to taste
1 cup grated Cheddar cheese

Preheat oven to 450 degrees. Place fries on baking sheet, sprinkle with Cajun seasoning, salt and pepper. Bake 10 minutes, top with grated cheese, bake until cheese is melted. Serve immediately.

FAT CONTENT RATING: 🐘 🐘 🐘 🐘

FILIBUSTERIN' FRENCH FRIES

Bill can eat these fries any ol' day for as long as any ol' windbag can hold up the Senate floor.

6 large Idaho potatoes, peeled
2 cups vegetable oil
Salt and pepper
Hot pepper flakes (optional)

FRIED:
Cut potatoes into slices and then into ½-inch strips. Immerse in cold water, pat dry.

Heat the oil until a drop of water sizzles. Add potatoes gently to oil, do not crowd. Fry to a golden brown. Drain on paper towels, salt and pepper to taste.

FAT CONTENT RATING: 🐘 🐘 🐘 🐘

BAKED:
Preheat oven to 450 degrees. Follow above directions but pour ¼ cup vegetable oil onto a large baking sheet. Put dried potatoes on sheet—be careful not to crowd. Bake turning frequently, approximately 12 to 15 minutes or until golden brown. Drain on paper towels. Season with salt and pepper to taste.

FAT CONTENT RATING: 🐘 🐘 🐘

"You get all the french fries the President can't get to."

–AL GORE, telling David Letterman the top ten best things about being vice president

HILLARY'S HUSHPUPPIES WITH SOMETHING FISHY

Ever since Bill and Hillary's dramatic live interview in the early days of the 1992 campaign, we've all known that the Clintons have worked hard at their marriage. In Hillary's book, *It Takes a Village*, she talks about the importance of staying married "till death do us part" instead of "until the going gets rough."

Apparently getting your love puppy to hush is a hallmark of Clinton marital strategy. "My strong feelings about divorce have caused me to bite my tongue more than a few times in my own marriage and to think instead about what I could do to be a better wife and partner. My husband has done the same," says Hil. What better than a plate of steaming hot hushpuppies to quiet an angry tongue and warm your loved one's heart?

FISH:
4 filets of sole or flounder
½ cup white cornmeal
Salt and pepper to taste
2 tablespoons vegetable oil

HUSHPUPPIES:
1½ cups white cornmeal
¼ cup all-purpose flour
1½ teaspoons baking powder
1 teaspoon baking soda
1 teaspoon salt
¾ teaspoon fresh pepper
1½ cups beer
4 scallions finely chopped

2 eggs
½ cup chopped red pepper
1 fresh jalapeño chili
1 cup vegetable oil

In a large bowl combine cornmeal, flour, baking powder, baking soda, salt and pepper. In another bowl stir together beer, eggs, scallions, red pepper and chili pepper.

Combine wet and dry ingredients.

Pour oil into heavy skillet. Heat until sizzling. Drop batter by tablespoonfuls and cook until browned and puffy. Turn and cook on other side. Remove from skillet and drain on paper towels.

Mix cornmeal, salt and pepper together. Dredge fish in mixture. Sauté in 2 tablespoons of vegetable oil for 3 minutes per side. Serve with hushpuppies.

FAT CONTENT RATING:

Doonesbury

BY GARRY TRUDEAU

THE WHITE HOUSE
WASHINGTON

January 5, 1951

Dear Owen:

I read your letter of the third with a lot of interest.

I've discussed the matter with the Secretary of Agriculture and he is trying to work something out. This potato problem has been rather a bad one to handle for the last few years. I hope we may be able to work it out in a satisfactory manner.

Sincerely yours,

Harry Truman

Honorable Owen Brewster
United States Senate
Washington, D. C.

Potato problem? What problem? Peel 'em, slice 'em, fry 'em and eat 'em!

Szathmary Family Culinary Collection JWU

PARMA PIEROGIES

The President was so impressed with the food at Parma Pierogies (potato, sauerkraut, apricot and cherry pierogies) in Cleveland, Ohio, and by the entrepreneurial good sense of the restaurant's owner and founder, Mary Poldruhi, that he invited her to his inauguration and named her one of his "Faces of Hope" in '94. Bill has eaten at the nation's first fast-food pierogi joint three times, and even takes nutritional advice from Poldruhi: "Quit going to those golden arches and come to a pierogi restaurant more often," she once reprimanded. And how did her honorable patron respond? "He said he was cutting back."

Makes 2½ to 3 dozen.

FOR THE DOUGH:
2 cups Montana Sapphire flour
Combine in ¾ cup measure:
   1 teaspoon salt
   1 egg or 2 egg yolks
   1 tablespoon oil
   Milk and/or water (if using both, one part of each) to equal ¾ cup

Add liquid mixture to flour; mix until blended. Knead on floured surface, adding flour until the dough is no longer sticky and looks smooth. Cover and let rest 15 minutes or overnight. Make fillings (recipes follow).

When ready to make pierogies, divide dough in half. Roll out to ⅛-inch thickness. Cut out circles with floured open end of glass. Put one tablespoon of filling in each and pinch together to make one layer out of two ends.

Cook about six at a time in boiling water about 5 minutes. Let water come to boil, drop pierogies in, cover 1 minute and remove cover. Stir with wooden spoon, cook uncovered three minutes, then cover for last minute while pierogies puff up and float to the top.*

Drain and sprinkle with melted butter.

TO FRY:
Heat 2 cups vegetable oil in a skillet until a drop of water sizzles on the surface. Gently place pierogies (do not crowd) in hot oil and fry for 2 to 3 minutes until golden.

Serve with melted butter or sour cream.

FAT CONTENT RATING:

*If you wish to freeze pierogies, let cook until warm. Put in Ziploc bag and freeze. When ready to eat, drop frozen pierogies into boiling water for about three minutes, until pierogies float to top.

PIEROGI FILLINGS

SAUERKRAUT FILLING:
2 medium onions chopped fine
4 tablespoons butter or bacon fat
2 16-ounce cans sauerkraut (boiled, drained, squeezed dry and chopped)
2 tablespoons bread crumbs

Cook onion in fat until tender. Add the sauerkraut, season mixture to taste and cook for 5 minutes. Add bread crumbs and mix well.

PRUNE FILLING:
Ready-to-eat pitted prunes can be used. Place one in each pierogi.

COTTAGE CHEESE FILLING:
1 carton (2 cups) dry cottage cheese
1 egg yolk, slightly beaten
2 tablespoons sugar

Combine ingredients, mix well.

POTATO FILLING:
5 large potatoes (3 cups hot mashed potatoes)
6 ounces cream cheese
2 ounces Cheddar or Swiss cheese (grated)
2 tablespoons melted butter
Salt and pepper to taste

Peel, cut and boil potatoes until soft. Mash potatoes and combine
with the remaining ingredients. Mix well.

IT'S A FORD

Often pressed by the more intellectual challenges of the job, Gerald Ford believed that "Eating and sleeping are a waste of time." He and his wife Betty would frequently dine out and order only martinis and salads.

CRISPY NEWTIE-O'S

The perfect rainy-day food, Crispy Newtie-O's are a great source of nutrition (tons of vitamin C in those onion rings) and they have a way of inspiring exercise. Like the Speaker himself, they're round and appealing on the outside, and just a touch slippery on the inside. They have great taste, but they're less filling, too. Serve these with Wild Bill Buffalo Burgers (page 22) or Gates's Good-Time Chili (page 18).

2 large Spanish onions
1½ cups all purpose flour
1 teaspoon salt
¼ teaspoon pepper
¼ teaspoon garlic powder
1 tablespoon vegetable oil
2 beaten egg yolks
a few shakes of Tabasco
¾ cup beer
2 stiffly beaten egg whites

Slice onions into ¼-inch rounds.

In a large bowl mix flour, salt, pepper, garlic powder, vegetable oil, egg yolks and Tabasco; gradually add beer.

Let rest 1 hour.

Add egg whites, mix and coat onions.

Heat oil in deep pot and fry until brown, drain on paper towels. Sprinkle with salt and pepper to taste.

FAT CONTENT RATING: 🐘 🐘 🐘 🐘 🐘

Playing
Chicken

The President often has to go head to head with his opponents, as the budget negotiations have demonstrated. Playing chicken, staring down the opposition until one of you backs down, is an accepted though frustrating part of political life. Eating chicken, on the other hand, is a more one-sided and therefore more satisfying enterprise.

Bill's love for chicken could be attributed to state pride. In the great state of Arkansas, about one billion birds are raised each year, and one out of every two people employed in the state works in the poultry trade. It's his duty to support his home state's biggest industry by eating as much chicken as he can, and he does his darndest to live up to that responsibility. Fortunately it's a versatile bird that can be dished up in a variety of ways that cover the fat spectrum, which is probably why it's so popular with the rest of us.

AMERICAN PIE

As a young lawyer, Abraham Lincoln kept up his strength and energy by eating fruit pies baked especially for him by the ladies of New Salem, Illinois. After he left for Washington, these ladies would ship fruit pies to the White House, decorated with steam gashes in the shapes of stars, letters indicating the type of fruit or "L" for Lincoln.

BUSHWACKIN' BROCCOLI CREAM CHICKEN

Cream of broccoli soup, broccoli with cheese sauce, deep-fried broccoli, broccoli corn bread—and for dessert, broccoli mousse…. Guess who's coming to dinner? That's right, it's the Bushes. George just can't seem to live down the disparaging remarks he made about broccoli back when he was the chief. And it doesn't help that both Bill and Chelsea have named George's evil green as their favorite vegetable.

3 cups cooked spaghetti
1½ cups steamed broccoli
2 cups cooked chicken
1 cup broccoli cheese soup
1 cup half-and-half or milk
½ teaspoon salt
¼ teaspoon pepper
1 cup shredded Cheddar cheese

In a casserole dish, combine cooked spaghetti, steamed broccoli and cooked chicken.

In a bowl, mix the broccoli cheese soup with the milk and salt and pepper.

Pour over the spaghetti and toss to mix. Top with grated Cheddar.

Bake at 350 degrees for 20 minutes or until bubbly and brown on top.

FAT CONTENT RATING: 🐘 🐘 🐘 🐘

LIZA'S HOT CHICKEN SALAD

When 32-year-old Bill Clinton took up residence in the Governor's Mansion in 1979, chef Liza Ashley was a bit intimidated by his youthful appetite. This salad is one of the first dishes she prepared for the Clintons. Though previous governors had favored casseroles and meatloafs, Liza easily took to the Clinton's favorite lamb, veal, fish and Mexican dishes. In her cookbook *Thirty Years at the Mansion*, Ashley says that cooking for Bill and Hil was easy, since they "didn't want to eat too much because they were afraid they'd get fat." Hmmm.

2 cups chicken, cooked and cut up
2 cups celery, cubed and cooked until tender
2 cups rice, cooked in chicken broth
2 cans cream of chicken soup
1¼ cups of mayonnaise
1 medium onion, chopped
6 tablespoons lemon juice
6 hard-boiled eggs, chopped
¾ cup slivered almonds
¼ cup butter, melted
1 cup crushed corn flakes

Preheat oven to 350 degrees. Prepare chicken, celery and rice. In a large bowl combine cream of chicken soup, mayonnaise, onion, lemon juice and chopped eggs. Add first 3 ingredients and mix well. Place in casserole for baking.

Heat almonds in melted butter and pour on top of casserole. Top with corn flakes. Bake for 45 minutes.

FAT CONTENT RATING: 🐘 🐘 🐘 🐘

In their rebuttal, the Republicans called for a smaller government. Of course, the President stood by his old claim that size doesn't matter.

–CONAN O'BRIEN

THE BUCK STOPS HEROES

The presidency is about taking responsibility. Though Bill may waffle from time to time, when the heroes are being passed around, the chain of command leads straight to the Oval Office. The President is known for craving all the worst foods when times are tense, so we can imagine a steady demand for these sandwiches and Bill's preferred Moosehead lager.

4 chicken breasts (skin on)
Vegetable oil
Salt and pepper to taste
1 cup mayonnaise
⅓ cup sliced canned jalapeño peppers
4 hero rolls (toasted)
4 scallions (sliced)
1 cup grated Cheddar cheese

Preheat oven to 400 degrees. Rub chicken breasts with vegetable oil, salt and pepper. Bake for 15 minutes. Let cool. Shred chicken into strips.

Combine mayonnaise and jalapeños in food processor. Grate cheese, chop scallions.

Toast rolls. Spread with jalapeño mayonnaise. Put chicken on rolls and top with scallions and cheese.

Grill until cheese is melted.

FAT CONTENT RATING: 🐘 🐘 🐘 🐘

"When the food came, the Governor inhaled his, then looked up shocked—and not undelighted—that the rest of us were still working, which left the possibility that more was to be had. He kept his eye on Susan's plate, then—at the instant she crumpled her last paper napkin—swiped the leftovers. He snagged my Texas toast when he thought no one was looking (he was wrong; Jimmy was). I was, for once, disappointed in him."
—Anonymous,
Primary Colors

FORGET FLOWERS FRIED CHICKEN

There's nothing like eating food that requires your full attention to help you forget what's best forgotten. Since idle hands are the devil's workshop, we suggest Bill dig into fried chicken the way it's meant to be eaten—the two-fisted way.

½ cup flour
2 tablespoons toasted sesame seeds
1 tablespoon baking soda
2 tablespoons paprika
2 eggs
½ cup milk
2 quarts vegetable oil
1 frying chicken, cut into parts

Mix dry ingredients in a large plastic bag. In a bowl beat eggs and mix with milk.

Soak chicken parts in egg mixture.

In a large pot heat 2 quarts of oil to 360 degrees. When oil is ready take out chicken parts and dredge in dry mixture by shaking it in the plastic bag.

When well covered place in the oil and cook for 15 minutes.

Drain on paper towels and serve.

FAT CONTENT RATING:

"The word was passed to get rid of all the booze. There can't be any on Air Force One, in Camp David, or in the White House. This was coming from close associates of the Carter family. I said to our White House military people, 'Hide the booze and let's find out what happens.' The first Sunday they are in the White House, I get a call from the mess saying, 'They want Bloody Marys before going to church. What should I do?' I said, 'Find some booze and take it up to them.'"

—BILL GULLY, chief of the White House Military Office, on Jimmy Carter's first days in office

BOMBAY CLUB'S CHICKEN TIKKA MAKHANI

O nce in a while, Bill likes to travel without having to get on board Air Force One. For a little taste of the Far East right in Washington, D.C., the President eats at the Bombay Club, where the food is generously spiced and the waiters pretend not to mind refilling his condiment tray every five minutes.

Basmati rice
2½ pounds boneless chunks of chicken

FOR THE MARINADE:
3 cups yogurt
1 tablespoon garlic and ginger paste*
¼ cup vegetable oil
2 cloves garlic, crushed
¼ teaspoon turmeric
1 teaspoon paprika
1 teaspoon Garam Masala

FOR THE SAUCE:
2 pounds chopped tomatoes
2 sticks butter
1 cup heavy cream
1 tablespoon honey
½ teaspoon curry powder
½ teaspoon salt

THE BOMBAY CLUB

Thread chicken onto bamboo skewers, about 6 pieces per skewer.

Combine marinade ingredients, mix well and marinate chicken in the refrigerator 6 to 8 hours.

Cook the tomatoes in the butter until soft. Purée in food processor or blender. Return to the pot and add the cream, honey, curry and salt. Bring to a boil, reduce heat and simmer approximately 10 minutes or until slightly reduced.

Grill or broil chicken approximately 5 minutes per side. Serve on a bed of Basmati rice and pour sauce over all.

*You can substitute garlic and ginger paste with tandoori paste, usually found in specialty food or health food stores. Garam Masala can be found at health food stores as well.

FAT CONTENT RATING:

oversized corned beef and pastrami sandwiches (the Vice President treated). Chernomyrdin ate with gusto and took the balance with him in a doggie bag as he headed off to the Waldorf-Astoria. He then went on to deliver perhaps the most concise and eloquent speech of his career, his trademark mumble replaced by a clear tone The New York Times called "calm, confident, almost lilting."

> "We would get warmed-over lasagna and two-day-old salad, the worst stuff I had since the Marines, and I never did see him complain. I suspect if they give it to him, he'll eat it. If the White House chef comes down with an elaborate duck à l'orange, he'll eat that, too."
>
> –JAMES CARVILLE, on eating airplane meals with Bill

CHARITY CHICKEN AND SAUSAGE GUMBO

Rubber chicken is a well-known staple of the speechmaking and fundraising circuits. If you want the President to attend your event, try including this piquant poultry on the menu.

6 ounces bacon
1 whole chicken, quartered
3 links hot and spicy sausage
½ cup corn
1 cup sliced okra
2 red peppers, diced
1 medium onion, diced
¼ cup rice
1 tablespoon Cajun spice
2 teaspoon salt
1 tablespoon filé gumbo powder

Cook bacon, leaving grease in pan. Cover the chicken quarters with flour and brown in bacon grease.

Boil 4 cups of water in a kettle. When chicken is browned add the water slowly, simmer until meat is cooked, approximately 30 minutes.

Pick meat from bones. Cook the sausage in a sauté pan; slice sausage and add to chicken.

To a pot of 3½ cups of water, mix in the corn, okra, peppers, onions, rice, bacon, Cajun spice, salt and filé gumbo powder.

Finally add the chicken and sausage.

Let the gumbo cook for 30 to 40 minutes before serving.

FAT CONTENT RATING: 🐘 🐘 🐘 🐘

Willie con Queso

Here's the Clinton Cheese Policy as best as we can figure: Bill is allergic to milk, but many of his favorite dishes feature cheese prominently. Now do you understand how he puts his other policies together? Lyndon Johnson also loved cheese in many of his favorite native dishes, such as tacos, chalupas and nachos. Chalupas were even served at a party for Lynda Johnson's bridesmaids in the Yellow Room.

But all of the people did not necessarily approve of all of these habits: the Johnson family cook, Zephyr Wright, offered up the following advice—which might help this administration as well: "Mr. President, you have been my boss for a number of years and you always tell me you want to lose weight and yet you never do very much to help yourself. Now I'm going to be your boss for a change. Eat what I put in front of you and don't ask for any more and don't complain."

ENDORSE-ME ENCHILADAS WITH SMOOTH-MELT CHEESE

B ill endorsed Liza Ashley's Chicken Enchiladas early in his gubernatorial days, and this recipe is based on the version that appears in Ashley's *Thirty Years at the Mansion*. Our candidate is more garlicky and adds extra seasoning. In a classic contradiction, though Clinton is allergic to dairy products, he somehow seems to be able to accommodate a bit of cheese in special dishes. In keeping with the platform of indulging the middle class, we couldn't bring ourselves to sacrifice a single shred of Cheddar.

Cooking oil
2 fresh jalapeño chilies
2 4-ounce cans green chilies
4 large garlic cloves, minced
1 28-ounce can tomatoes
2 cups chopped onion
2 teaspoons salt
1½ teaspoons oregano
3 cups shredded cooked chicken
2½ cups sour cream
2½ cups grated Cheddar cheese
15 flour tortillas
1½ cups smooth-melt cheese
½ cup chopped fresh cilantro

Preheat 2 tablespoons oil in skillet. Chop chilies after removing seeds; sauté with minced garlic in oil.

Reserving ½ cup liquid, drain and break up tomatoes. To chilies and garlic add tomatoes, onion, 1 teaspoon salt, oregano and reserved tomato liquid.

Simmer uncovered until thick, about 30 minutes. Remove from skillet and set aside.

Combine chicken with sour cream, grated cheese and remaining salt.

Heat ⅓ cup of oil. Fry tortillas briefly in oil until they become limp. *Do not crisp up.* Drain well on paper towels. Fill tortillas with chicken mixture; roll up and arrange side by side, seam down, in 9x13x2-inch baking dish. Pour chili sauce over enchiladas and slice smooth-melt cheese and layer on top. Bake at 350 degrees until heated through, about 20 minutes. Sprinkle cilantro on top before serving.

FAT CONTENT RATING: 🐘 🐘 🐘

HOT TICKET TAMALES

Bill's mom, Virginia Clinton Kelley, knew where to find the best tamales in Little Rock, and possibly the best in the world. Virginia was a regular customer at Margie Allen's "tamale trailer," a mobile food vendor that used to deliver steaming hot tamales to the corner outside the capitol building and that can still be found on weekends in the parking lot of Yancy's liquors at Cavanaugh Street. Margie started up her business about 11 years ago with a tamale recipe she got from the back of a package of corn shucks at the Food King. The Allen family (son Micky now drives the trailer) has since added many personal touches to that recipe, which now officially qualifies as a family secret. According to Margie, corn husks are too costly to buy in quantity at the grocery store (they cost about $3.50 a packet), so her daughter buys them by the bale in Texas and the two meet in Texarkana, halfway between their respective homes, for the hand-off. Our tamale recipe uses Masa Harina instead of the costly shucks. You can find Masa Harina in the Mexican food section of your grocery store.

FOR THE FILLING:
1½ pounds flank steak
4 cups water
1 onion stuck with 5 whole cloves
½ head garlic, cut in half (peel on)
3 bay leaves
½ teaspoon salt

FOR THE FILLING SAUCE:
4 tablespoons olive oil
1 medium onion, chopped
8 garlic cloves, minced
½ pound spicy sausage

3 large tomatoes, roasted
4 dried chipotle chilies, fried
2 bay leaves
⅓ cup vinegar
2 tablespoons brown sugar
2 dashes cinnamon
salt and pepper
water

FOR THE DOUGH:
12 ounces prepared Masa Harina
1½ cups boiling water
½ cup cornstarch
1 teaspoon baking powder
1 teaspoon salt
½ pound lard
1 package parchment paper or aluminum foil

FILLING:
Place all ingredients in a heavy saucepan and simmer on low heat, approximately 1½ hours, adding more water as necessary. Cook until meat is very tender. Shred flank steak and add to sauce.

FILLING SAUCE:
Heat oil in pan; sauté onion and garlic. Add sausage, tomatoes, chipotles; sauté 2 minutes.
    Add bay leaves, vinegar, brown sugar, cinnamon, salt and pepper. Cook until mixture thickens, add water as necessary. Remove bay leaves.

DOUGH:
Place Masa Harina in a large bowl. Add boiling water gradually and knead until it's no longer sticky. Add cornstarch, baking powder and

salt. In another bowl beat the lard with an electric mixer until it is light and fluffy (about 5 minutes).

Work lard into Masa mixture with your hands, kneading thoroughly. Test for lightness by dropping a piece into a glass of cold water; if it floats it's light enough—if not, continue kneading.

FINAL ASSEMBLY:
Cut out a rectangle of parchment paper about 6x8 inches; spread some of the dough in the middle.

Top with the meat mixture, cover with more dough and roll up into a log shape, twisting the ends of the paper to seal.

Place in a steamer and steam for approximately 1 hour. Keep adding water to the steamer so it doesn't boil dry. Serve with Hot Tamale Sauce (recipe follows). Bill loves them!

FAT CONTENT RATING: 🐘 🐘 🐘 🐘 (with sauce)

HOT TAMALE SAUCE

1 cup beef broth
⅓ cup crushed tomatoes
¼ cup dried chipotle chilies
¼ cup red wine
1 tablespoon brown sugar
¼ teaspoon cumin
1 clove garlic, minced
½ teaspoon salt
Masa dough to thicken

Combine above ingredients in saucepan, cook together approximately 10 minutes, add extra Masa dough to thicken as needed.

Serve over hot tamales.

THE KITCHENGATE SCANDAL

Shortly after the Clintons moved into 1600 Pennsylvania Avenue, an elite delegation from the American Society of Culinary Art commenced lobbying Bill and Hillary to fire the White House executive chef, Pierre Chambrin, and hire an American chef.

"I call it a three-way taste bud battle," said Dian McLellan, social columnist. "There's the rich French cuisine versus nouvelle American and Bubba Grub. They were all on a collision course—and the number one casualty was French."

Chambrin, who had been White House executive chef since 1990, was fired, but, "It's not my deal," said Clinton, when asked about Chambrin's departure at a press conference. "I'm an indiscriminate eater. I don't know anything about it."

The new chef, Walter Scheib III, serves American-style entrées for state dinners, and provides the First Family with healthy meals that, he claims, are "indistinguishable from normal food."

AS YE SOW

On one of his elephantine eating binges, Bill Clinton was on his way to lunch with two senators at an Ohio restaurant when he spotted a roadside café called Charlie's House of Meats. He jumped from his limousine and wolfed down a large apple fritter while waiting for a burger with cheese. This little snack did not stop him from polishing off a large pastrami sandwich and cream cheese pastry with the senators. Afterwards, he told the restaurant owner he felt "like a sow in the sun" and needed to take a nap.

"Chili concocted outside of Texas is usually a weak, apologetic imitation of the real thing. One of the first things I do when I get home to Texas is have a bowl of red. There is simply nothing better."

—LYNDON JOHNSON

CHILI CON QUESO

Everybody's got a chili recipe these days—senators, rock stars, debutantes and television hosts are just a few who love the hot stuff enough to copyright their own versions. Since Bill doesn't have a lot of free time on his hands, we decided to create a recipe just for him that would borrow from a few of his favorite things: Mexican food, beef, cheese, beans, tomatoes, onions, peppers, garlic.... We'll stop there, except to say that Bill's late mother Virginia Kelley can be thanked for instilling her son with a proper respect for a good bowl of red. Virginia, who once judged at the Saratoga Regional Chili Cookoff, would surely approve of this comfortably spicy concoction.

2 tablespoons vegetable oil
2 medium onions, chopped
2 green peppers, chopped
3 large cloves garlic, minced
1½ pounds ground beef
1 chili seasoning packet
1 15-ounce can peeled tomatoes
1 15-ounce can red kidney beans
2 cups grated Cheddar cheese
sour cream

Heat oil in sauté pan. Add chopped onions, peppers and minced garlic. Sauté until tender. Add ground beef and brown.

Add chili seasoning packet and mix well with meat and onions. Add tomatoes and kidney beans.

Simmer together until thickened, approximately 20 to 25 minutes. Serve with grated Cheddar cheese and a dollop of sour cream.

FAT CONTENT RATING:

NEW DEAL NACHOS

Franklin D. Roosevelt's New Deal changed the direction of social legislation, centralized the country's economic power and transformed the role of the federal government. Bill's North American Free Trade Agreement can't exactly boast such sweeping changes, but at least Clinton has helped to mold a new way of dealing with our neighbors. No doubt his weakness for Mexican food had nothing to do with the push to pass this legislation, but we can imagine the White House staff celebrated the signing of NAFTA with a plate of Mexican tortilla chips, garnished American-style.

1 pound ground beef
1 packet taco seasoning mix
Large bag nacho corn chips
1 12-ounce jar medium-hot salsa
1 finely chopped onion
5 ounces sliced jalapeño peppers
1 can sliced black olives
2 cups Monterey Jack cheese
1 cup Cheddar cheese
⅓ cup sour cream
4 chopped scallions
Salt and pepper to taste

Cook beef in large skillet; drain grease and stir in taco seasoning.

Spread corn chips in 12x20-inch sheet pan. Layer beef, salsa, onions, jalapeños and olives on top of chips. Sprinkle cheese evenly over dish.

Place 6 inches under broiler for 8 minutes or until cheese is melted.

Garnish with sour cream and scallions.

FAT CONTENT RATING: 🐘 🐘 🐘 🐘

THE KISSINGER KISS-OFF

According to the chief steward on Air Force One, "Henry Kissinger... didn't like peas. If there were peas on his plate, he would take a knife and brush them on the floor. He was a real messy eater. There were a lot of things on the floor before he was finished." Shocking.

CHILI RELLENOS

L ike a lot of issues Bill has to deal with every day, these chilies are too hot to handle. They require statesmanship—give them the kid glove treatment and cover them with a more moderate dressing to make them go down easier.

½ cup vegetable oil
6 large Poblano chilies
½ cup raisins
3 tablespoons butter
2 large garlic cloves, minced
1 small onion, finely chopped
1 cup converted rice
2½ cups water
½ cup slivered almonds
¼ cup sliced green olives
¼ cup chopped cilantro
6 ounces white Cheddar cheese, grated
½ teaspoon cumin
½ teaspoon salt

Fry chilies in large sauté pan (get oil very hot first) until puffed and beige colored. Carefully (using rubber gloves) peel chilies and remove seeds.

Plump raisins in boiling water about 20 minutes.

Heat 2 tablespoons of the butter in saucepan; add garlic and onion, cook until translucent. Add rice and cook 2 minutes. Add the water and bring to a boil then reduce heat to low; cover pan and simmer for 20 minutes.

Preheat oven to 350 degrees. Sauté almonds in remaining 1 tablespoon of butter until golden and fragrant. To cooked rice mixture add almonds, olives, cilantro, raisins, cheese, cumin and salt.

Stuff each chili and place in medium-sized casserole dish.

Cover with Roasted Tomato-Garlic Sauce (recipe follows) and bake 15 minutes or until heated through.

FAT CONTENT RATING: 🐘 🐘 🐘 🐘 🐘 (with sauce)

ROASTED TOMATO-GARLIC SAUCE

1½ cups heavy cream
10 large garlic cloves, unpeeled
1 onion, unpeeled and cut in half
3 pounds very ripe tomatoes
Salt and pepper
Hot pepper flakes to taste

Cook down cream in small saucepan over low to medium heat until reduced by one-third.

Heat a very large skillet; roast the unpeeled garlic cloves and halved onion until softened and blackened.

Roast tomatoes the same way, turning until blistered on all sides. Let cool slightly.

Peel garlic and onion; blend in food processor with salt, pepper and hot pepper flakes.

Peel tomatoes; add to onion mixture in processor.

Add reduced cream; process till smooth.

"Recently President Clinton went jogging in Israel along the West Bank. His thighs were so white the Palestinians thought he was surrendering."

–DAVID LETTERMAN

"Officials are debating whether the guy who shot at the White House was really trying to kill the President or was just shooting randomly. You gotta figure that if he was really trying to kill Clinton, he would have shot at the kitchen window."

—DENNIS MILLER

LAYERED TACO DIP

A good politician must have multiple layers, just like a good taco dip. He or she must be as hearty as refried beans at the core, gloriously cheesy on the surface and stacked in between with fresh ingredients and lots of spice.

2 avocados
2 tablespoons lime juice
½ teaspoon of ground cumin
½ teaspoon of salt
1 package taco seasoning mix
½ cup mayonnaise
8 ounces sour cream
1 can refried beans
2 or 3 tomatoes, chopped
1 bunch scallions, chopped
1 can pitted black olives chopped in food processor
8 ounces Cheddar cheese, shredded

Mash avocados in food processor with lime juice, cumin and salt.

Combine taco seasoning mix with mayonnaise and sour cream.

Spread refried beans over the bottom of a 9x13x2-inch baking dish. Layer avocado mixture on top, followed by mayonnaise mixture. Layer remaining ingredients in the order given.

Serve with tortilla chips.

FAT CONTENT RATING:

Slick Sneakin' Food

What transforms mild-mannered Bill Clinton into the infamous Slick Willie? Is it his silvery tongue or the greasy food that he slides down his gullet with the greatest of ease? And what we do we really prefer in a president, Teflon or good old-fashioned butter and oil?

These are the hard questions that this chapter makes us examine. Before you cast your first vote—or stone—bear in the mind that according to the Snack Food Association, last year we the American people consumed 5.7 billion pounds of salty snack foods like potato chips, popcorn, pretzels, cheese puffs, tortilla chips, nuts and beef jerky—about 22 pounds for every man, woman and child in the country.

SOCKS'S TUNA AND CHEESE MELT

The next time Socks mews in complaint about her unsavory diet of dry catfood and being unceremoniously asked to sleep outside at night (Bill is allergic to cat hair), perhaps Chelsea will offer her deserving feline friend the Tuna and Cheese Melt we created in the First Kitty's honor—or at least the tuna part of it.

After all, the pets of past presidents have certainly led far more decadent lives than the oft-photographed Socks. President Taft loved fresh milk so much that he kept a Holstein named Pauline Wayne on the White House grounds and even hired a man exclusively to milk and care for her. And during World War I, President Woodrow Wilson kept a flock of sheep to trim the White House lawns while the gardeners were off fighting the war. One of the rams went by the name of Old Ike and had a tobacco chewing habit. Old Ike was rarely seen without brown juices running down his chin, but was polite enough not to spit his chew out on the well-cropped White House lawn. As for other eccentric animal indulgences: President Coolidge, whose love of animals turned 1600 Pennsylvania Avenue into a veritable zoo, once poured a saucer of coffee for his dog Blake during a breakfast with fellow politicians. Johnson vowed to keep his hounds (virtually his only loyal supporters during the Vietnam War) healthy by feeding them candy-coated vitamin pills.

4 English muffins, split
1 6-ounce can tuna, drained and flaked
1 cup shredded yellow Cheddar cheese
¼ cup minced green or red peppers
2 tablespoons minced onion
½ cup mayonnaise

Toast muffins. Mix remaining ingredients well and place on muffins, making open-faced sandwiches.

Place under broiler 5 minutes or until lightly browned. Transfer to a bowl and serve on the floor.

FAT CONTENT RATING: 🐘 🐘

LATE-NIGHT SPAGHETTI OMELET

"Hillary's actually a pretty good cook, and I actually like to cook, but what I like to do is make things like omelets. Sometimes on Sunday nights, Hillary and Chelsea and I will go into the kitchen and I'll make everybody omelets and we'll sit around and talk." So says the President. Let's give them something to talk about.

3 eggs
2 tablespoons heavy cream
1 tablespoon butter (to grease pan)
½ cup leftover spaghetti with sauce
3 tablespoons grated Parmesan cheese

The key to a good omelet is not to overbeat the eggs.

In a bowl combine eggs and cream. With a fork lightly beat the eggs just enough to break the yolks. In a small frying pan or omelet pan melt butter.

Be sure to cover the entire surface with butter. When pan is hot, pour in the eggs. Let eggs cook until almost dry. Add leftover spaghetti and Parmesan to omelet, flip omelet over on top of spaghetti and serve.

FAT CONTENT RATING:

CAMPAIGN TRAIL MIX

One presidential late-night snack reportedly consists of cocktail shrimp, pastries, mango sorbet and French bread dripping with olive oil. Maybe now you understand how that health care plan came together. Unfortunately, when Bill's on the campaign trail, the pickings are considerably slimmer, but this handy snack would get the President through those early morning hours, when he's said to be most prone to the snacking urge.

1 1-pound bag plain M&M's (must have presidential blue ones!)
1 pound salted dry roasted peanuts
1 15-ounce box of raisins
1 pound sunflower seeds

Mix above ingredients together in a paper bag. Store in a cool dry place.

FAT CONTENT RATING: 🐘 🐘 🐘 🐘

TIPPER'S MAYONNAISE AND POTATO CHIP SANDWICHES

Here is Tipper Gore's most celebrated snack—guaranteed good, clean fun. We couldn't make this up if we tried. And no "Parental Advisory" is needed while the kids make these. If only Pat Boone, Amy Grant and Debbie Gibson sounded as good as mayo, white bread and potato chips taste, Tip's ideal world wouldn't be such a bad place.

8 slices firm white bread
4 tablespoons of mayonnaise
1 bag rippled potato chips
Lettuce (optional)

Spread mayonnaise on bread, top with chips and lettuce.

FAT CONTENT RATING: 🐘 🐘 🐘 🐘 🐘

DON'T-ASK-DON'T-TELL-RO-TEL SNACK

BILL ATE HERE · BILL ATE HERE

One can imagine that the Clinton policy on gays in the military was a clever adaptation of his desired policy on dietary discussions with Hillary. This snack is a Little Rock favorite of Bill's that's as easy to make as it is on the stomach, unless you're allergic to milk, like the President. But then cheese doesn't really count, now does it?

1 pound smooth-melt cheese
1 10-ounce can Ro-tel tomatoes and green chilies
or
1 10-ounce can stewed tomatoes and 1 4-ounce can green chilies
½ can sliced ripe olives
Tortilla chips or crackers

Cut cheese up into cubes. Put cheese, tomatoes, chilies and olives together in a covered glass casserole dish. Microwave 5 minutes on high power until cheese is melted. Let cool 2 minutes. Stir once and serve with tortilla chips or crackers.

FAT CONTENT RATING: 🐘 🐘 🐘

HISTORY OF THE BIG CHEESE

Bill isn't the first president to know cheese. In 1801, Thomas Jefferson received a block that weighed in at 1,600 pounds and had traveled from New England to Washington by sleigh. Two years later, the same cheese was still showing up on the plates of White House guests. Andrew Jackson received a similar but slightly smaller gift of cheese that weighed in at 1,400 pounds. But President Jackson and his friends made much shorter work of their block, apparently polishing off the whole thing at a reception in under 2 hours, leaving behind only a lingering aroma that was reportedly difficult to flush from the White House.

WORLD
DOMIN-O-
ATION

*According to
Domino's, pizza
orders by the White
House are 30% higher
now than during the
Bush administration,
and the average flow
of pies to 1600
Pennsylvania Avenue
increases by 18%
when Hillary is out of
town.*

PITFALL PIZZAS

"You can pretty much tell the state of the nation by how many he eats," says Jim Czarnecki, manager of the K Street branch of Domino's Pizza in Washington. In September of 1994, as the crisis in Haiti floundered towards a climax and the 82nd Airborne Division droned its way towards the terrorized country, the looming question in the White House briefing room was whether General Cedres's army would surrender to the U.S. threat before President Clinton surrendered to his hunger. At 6:30 p.m., the President took action: he picked up the phone and ordered a large veggie pizza with broccoli. Truth is that Clinton prefers his pizzas with sausage or pepperoni, but Hillary has laid down a clear embargo. But even with vegetables on top, Clinton craves pie when under stress.

1 10-ounce bake-and-roll pizza crust
or
1 12-inch frozen prepared pizza crust
1 cup spaghetti sauce
2 tablespoons olive oil

Preheat oven to 425 degrees. Press out dough into a greased 12-inch pizza pan. Spread with spaghetti sauce. Sprinkle with olive oil and top with any of the following combinations:

#1
¾ cup crumbled, cooked sweet sausage
½ cup grated Mozzarella cheese
½ cup grated Parmesan cheese

#2
¾ cup Mexican salsa
¾ cup sour cream
¾ cup grated Monterey Jack cheese

#3
1 cup grated Swiss cheese
¾ cup sliced ham
1 thinly sliced red onion

#4
1 cup crumbled feta cheese
¾ cup sliced olives
¼ cup sliced hot peppers
1 teaspoon oregano

Bake pizza approximately 15 to
20 minutes or until crust is
golden and cheese is bubbling.

FAT CONTENT RATING:

*One of Jimmy Carter's
favorites, a dish after Bill's
heart, with fat-laden
ingredients and hot spices.*

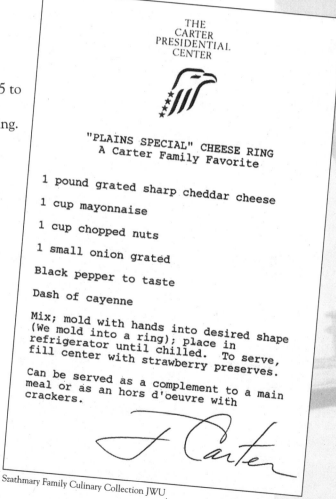

THE
CARTER
PRESIDENTIAL
CENTER

"PLAINS SPECIAL" CHEESE RING
A Carter Family Favorite

1 pound grated sharp cheddar cheese

1 cup mayonnaise

1 cup chopped nuts

1 small onion grated

Black pepper to taste

Dash of cayenne

Mix; mold with hands into desired shape
(We mold into a ring); place in
refrigerator until chilled. To serve,
fill center with strawberry preserves.

Can be served as a complement to a main
meal or as an hors d'oeuvre with
crackers.

Szathmary Family Culinary Collection JWU

Hillary's Obligatory Vegetable Chapter

"The good news is, my husband loves to eat and enjoys it. The bad news is, he loves to eat, even when things are not always right for him."

—HILLARY

The simple truth is, Hillary made us put this chapter here. And what Hil wants, Hil gets. The more complex truth is that even Bill has found a way to make vegetables tasty occasionally. So give his program a chance—you may be pleasantly surprised.

GRILLED ISLAND VEGETABLES WITH PASTA SALAD

Here's a dish chef V. Jaime Hamlin Schilcher often prepares when catering birthday dinners and weddings. It's light, 100% vegetarian and made from hearty vegetables so a little goes a long way—perhaps not long enough for Bill, though. This popular item was not requested when Schilcher catered Bill's 47th birthday party, where the five hearty courses included Codfish Cakes, Corn Pudding, Beefsteak Tomato Salad, Local Vineyard Swordfish and Lemon Poppy Seed Cake.

2 pounds zucchini
2 pounds summer squash
3 red peppers
1 large eggplant
4 ounces fresh mushrooms
3 leeks
1 1-pound package linguine

FOR THE MARINADE:
½ cup soy sauce
¼ cup olive oil
3 cloves minced garlic

Mix marinade ingredients together. Cut zucchini, squash and peppers into thick strips. Cut up eggplant into ¼-inch half-moon rounds. Halve mushrooms; halve leeks and wash thoroughly.

Pour marinade over vegetables.

Preheat oven to 400 degrees. Put vegetables in a baking pan; bake for 30 minutes or until tender and browned.

Boil linguine according to directions. Pour vegetables over and serve.

FAT CONTENT RATING:

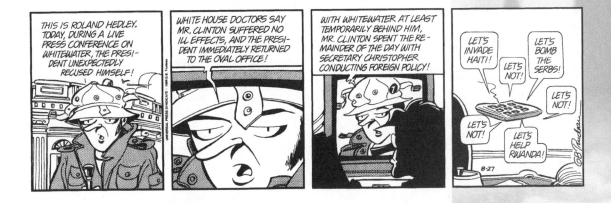

VIRGINIA'S SWEET POTATO

The beloved foods of childhood are often the ones we crave for life, and when Momma Virginia wanted to take care of her little sweet potato she knew the way to his heart was through his stomach. Nothing made Bill shake, rattle and roll like sweet potatoes, and this sweetly savory casserole remains a Clinton favorite.

6 pounds mashed sweet potatoes
½ pound (2 sticks) butter
3 eggs
1 pound brown sugar
1½ cups sweetened condensed milk
⅛ teaspoon nutmeg
¼ teaspoon cinnamon
2 teaspoons vanilla extract
¼ teaspoon ginger
½ teaspoon allspice
1 cup chopped pecans (roasted 4 minutes in a 375-degree toaster oven)
10 ounces mini-marshmallows

Wash, peel and thinly slice sweet potatoes. Boil in salted water to cover, approximately 10 to 15 minutes or until tender. Drain and return to pot. Add butter and mash thoroughly using electric mixer or potato masher. Add eggs, brown sugar and condensed milk. Mix thoroughly and blend in remaining ingredients, except mini-marshmallows. Put in a casserole and spread mini-marshmallows over the top of the casserole.

Broil approximately 2 minutes before serving to melt marshmallows.

FAT CONTENT RATING:

AL'S ORGANIC OKRA AND TANGY TOMATOES

Like any good Veep, Al's job is to balance the ticket. Bill is loose, Al is stiff; Bill likes to rock, Al likes to roll; Bill's wife defends children, Al's wife defends the language. But most importantly, Al is the Green Guy. So this one's for him: all natural, all organic, all the way to 2000 and beyond. (Make sure to prepare this with a wooden spoon.)

2 tablespoons butter
1 clove garlic, finely chopped
½ cup finely chopped onion
½ cup finely chopped green pepper
2 cups okra, cut into ½-inch slices (can use frozen okra)
1 cup chopped peeled fresh tomatoes
⅛ teaspoon oregano
Salt and pepper to taste

In a large skillet, sauté the garlic, onion and green pepper in butter until tender but not browned. Add the okra and cook 5 minutes, stirring frequently.

Add the tomatoes and oregano. Cover and simmer 10 minutes. Season to taste with salt and pepper and serve hot.

FAT CONTENT RATING:

GEORGE FOOLED

Clinton aide George Stephanopoulos loves to tell the story of how he learned that nothing can be taken for granted in the White House. One evening as he chatted with Bill and Al in the Chief's private dining room, a steward arrived with two trays. One had baked swordfish, a dried-out baked potato and green beans; the other, a Mexican Fiesta Platter, loaded with tacos, enchiladas, rice and beans. Of course, there was much laughter from the aides, because everyone was certain about who ordered what. But this time Bill had the last laugh. "The truth was that Clinton ate the swordfish," Mr. Stephanopoulos said. "I was as surprised as anyone."

TRIO'S SPINACH DIP WITH PEPPERY PITA CHIPS

Sure, this dip is largely made from cheese and cream, but that doesn't stop Bill from counting it as the "green" portion of his (ahem) balanced diet. Trio's, in Little Rock, has been feeding Bill their Spinach Dip for years. Clinton loves it so much, in fact, that in his first days at the White House he made sure his transition team was stocked with a steady supply, ordering as much as four gallons on a single day.

FOR THE SPINACH DIP:
1 10-ounce package chopped frozen spinach, thawed and squeezed dry
2 cups grated Monterey Jack cheese
1 8-ounce package cream cheese, softened
2 small yellow onions, chopped (1½ to 2 cups)
2 tablespoons chopped pickled jalapeño pepper, or to taste
⅓ cup half-and-half
2 cups canned, seeded, diced tomatoes, well drained

FOR THE PITA CHIPS:
6 pita rounds
2 sticks butter
cumin
lemon-pepper seasoning

FOR THE SPINACH DIP:
Preheat oven to 350 degrees. Thoroughly blend together all ingredi-

ents except tomato. (Use slow speed on mixer with paddle or batter attachment, or a wooden spoon or hands.) Add tomatoes, stir well. Put mixture into ovenproof casserole and bake for about 20 minutes or until hot and bubbly.

Serve with pita chips.

FOR THE PITA CHIPS:
Cut each pita round into 8 triangles. Brush pita triangles with melted butter and season with cumin and lemon pepper seasoning. Bake in 350-degree oven for 15 to 20 minutes or until crispy.

FAT CONTENT RATING: 🐘 🐘 🐘

An inventory of china unpacked by George Washington, written in his own hand.

Szathmary Family Culinary Collection JWU

BUSH-LEAGUE BROCCOLI CHEESE CORN BREAD

"I do not like broccoli, and I haven't liked it since I was a little kid and my mother made me eat it. And I'm President of the United States, and I'm not going to eat any more broccoli." It was this proclamation from President George Bush that angered farmers enough to dump truckloads of the vegetable in front of the White House in protest. The bushy green many Americans love to hate had become the most controversial crucifer in history. And when Bill won the presidential seat in '92, one of the first questions asked of him by the press was: "What's the word on broccoli?" It turns out that it's one of the few vegetables that Clinton supports whole-heartedly. For those Americans who still flip-flop on their personal position, here's a recipe that hides the goodness of broccoli within a tasty bread.

2½ cups yellow cornmeal
1 cup all-purpose flour
2 tablespoons sugar
2 tablespoons salt
4 teaspoons baking powder
½ cup nonfat dry milk
3 eggs at room temperature
1½ cups warm water (110 degrees)
1½ cup cooking oil
1 1-pound can creamy-style corn
5 jalapeño chili peppers, chopped
2 cups sharp Cheddar cheese, grated

1 large onion, grated
1 cup steamed broccoli, chopped

Preheat oven to 425 degrees. Spray one 10x15-inch glass pan with nonstick cooking spray.

In a large bowl stir together the cornmeal, flour, sugar, salt, baking powder and dry milk. In a smaller bowl lightly beat the eggs and stir in water and oil. Pour the liquid mixture into the cornmeal mix and stir in the corn, the chopped peppers, cheese, onion and broccoli.

Pour the batter into the baking pans and spread evenly with a rubber scraper or wooden spoon.

Bake for 30 minutes or until a wooden toothpick or metal skewer inserted in the center comes out clean.

FAT CONTENT RATING:

MEAL-POLITIK

"There's no spa cuisine here," bragged Filomena's chef Vito Piazza after Bill lunched on his fare with Chancellor Helmut Kohl of Germany. "Our motto is abbondanza." The indulgences went as follows: Cold antipasto of meats and cheeses, a hot antipasto of mushrooms stuffed with crabmeat, battered shrimp in orange sauce, fried calamari, a Tuscan soup with white beans and tomato, a main course of ravioli stuffed with veal, cheese and spinach and generous portions of a cholesterol lover's zabaglione. Government experts estimated the total calorie count at 3,400 (and if those are the same experts who project the budget deficit, you can only imagine what the real count was).

HILLARY'S BEIJING STIR-FRY

The First Lady made waves when she spoke out for women's rights at a conference in Beijing in the spring of '95. (Some thought her appearance conflicted with the U.S. boycott of China over human rights issues.) The conference was a success, and Hillary returned to the White House emboldened, asserting herself more freely with Bill by making him eat more stir-fries and fewer pies.

1 red pepper
1 zucchini
1 yellow squash
4 scallions
8 ounces sliced mushrooms
4 tablespoons olive oil
2 cloves garlic, minced
3 tablespoons soy sauce

Start by cutting vegetables. Cut red peppers in thin strips lengthwise. Slice zucchini into thin rounds then cut the rounds in half. Do the same with the yellow squash. Cut the scallions 2 inches up from the root and thinly chop. Slice the mushrooms into thin sections.

In a large frying pan, heat olive oil. Once oil is hot, add garlic. The order in which the vegetables are cooked is important because they all require different cooking times.

Start with the pepper, zucchini and squash. The scallions and mushrooms should not be cooked as long as the rest of the vegetables. Add the soy sauce with the scallions and mushrooms. When the vegetables are tender, take off heat and serve plain or on top of instant white rice.

FAT CONTENT RATING:

Monkey Business

"At a town meeting in Rhode Island, President Clinton said that there are powerful forces threatening to bring down his administration. Yeah, I think they're called hormones."

—JAY LENO

"Bob Dole accused President Clinton of pushing too much, too hard, too quickly. Ohh, I'm sorry... that was Paula Jones."

—CONAN O'BRIEN

"That means he's busy eating fast food, chasing women and giving Bob Dole the finger."

—DAVID LETTERMAN,
on Gore filling in while Clinton is on vacation

I s it a surprise to anyone that Bill is crazy for bananas? The fruit, that is. (Pat Nixon loved them, too.) A healthy addition to any kind of pudding, pie, bread, or even sandwich (after all, the government's food pyramid calls for five fruit servings a day), this monkey business will never bring an elected official down.

BUTTERED-UP BRANDY BANANA PUDDING

Bill's not a complete teetotaler, but he does prefer water or soda to wine at dinner, and even drinks nonalcoholic beer. That's why this concoction of bananas and brandy may be a danger to the female celebrity sitting next to him at one of those White House "soirées." Try it yourself and you'll understand why brandy makes Bill randy—the proof is in the puddin'.

3 bananas
1 cup heavy cream
4 eggs
1 tablespoon vanilla extract
1 cup brown sugar
2 tablespoons brandy
½ teaspoon salt
6 slices buttered white bread
½ teaspoon nutmeg

Preheat oven to 350 degrees. Thinly slice the bananas. In a medium mixing bowl beat together cream, eggs, vanilla, ¾ cup brown sugar, brandy and salt.

Cut buttered bread into quarters. Grease soufflé dish with non-stick cooking spray. Place a layer of bread pieces on bottom, then top with a layer of banana slices. Sprinkle with brown sugar and nutmeg. Continue layering in this fashion until all bread pieces and banana slices are used. Pour the cream-egg-brandy mixture over the top, and sprinkle with brown sugar. Bake for 1 hour.

Serve warm with whipped cream.

FAT CONTENT RATING:

GRILLED ELVISES

When the Elvis Presley commemorative stamp went on sale at Graceland eight hours before its availability at the U.S. Post Office, Bill had a man in line to buy out what is rumored to be several hundred of the stamps. One wonders if it was Elvis's music that moved the President so, or if it was the King's love of peanut butter and banana sandwiches.

½ cup crunchy peanut butter
2 very ripe bananas
8 slices Pepperidge Farm white bread
1 tablespoon butter
1½ tablespoons brown sugar

Blend the peanut butter with the banana until creamy. Spread the mixture on 4 slices of bread. Top with the remaining bread.

In a skillet melt enough butter to coat the bottom of the pan. Add brown sugar. Place the sandwiches in the butter and grill them until the bread is lightly toasted. Flip to grill the other side.

Drain on paper towels.

FAT CONTENT RATING:

"President Clinton said on his second anniversary in office, 'I am proud of the action I have taken, and I am also proud of the action I have gotten.'"

—JAY LENO

BANANA CREAM PIE

Bill Clinton's campaign bus had a "last banana" rule, according to one of his aides. No one except Clinton was to eat the last banana. Here's a rich, creamy pie he can make himself when he's down to his last banana.

1 egg white
1 premade graham cracker pie crust
1 banana
2 cups milk
1 box instant vanilla pudding
¼ teaspoon vanilla extract

Preheat oven to 350 degrees. Beat egg white and brush on pie crust. Bake for 8 minutes. Take out and let cool.

Cut banana in half; slice one half into rounds and set aside. In a mixing bowl, mash the other half with a fork.

Add milk, vanilla extract and pudding mix, blend with electric mixer. Pour into pie crust; let pudding set.

Top with banana rounds for garnish.

FAT CONTENT RATING:

BILL'S BUDGET PECAN BANANA BREAD

Q: *What's cheaper than a banana?*

A: *A Republican balancing the budget.*

After months of tug-of-war with Republicans over the dwindling federal budget, Bill doesn't want any arguments with Hillary over how much to spend on dessert.

½ cup butter
¾ cup brown sugar
3 cups mashed bananas
2 eggs beaten
1½ cups all-purpose flour
1 teaspoon baking powder
1 teaspoon salt
1 cup chopped pecans

Preheat oven to 300 degrees. Cream butter and sugar, add bananas, eggs and dry ingredients, mixing only enough to moisten.

Put into greased 8x4-inch loaf pan. Bake for 1½ hours or until toothpick comes out clean.

FAT CONTENT RATING: 🐘

"*I'm always happy to see him enjoying his food. I think it's terribly important. There is so much fear of food around and people are not enjoying it enough.*"

–JULIA CHILD

Let Them Eat Cake

When Marie Antoinette advocated spreading the desserts around, she had the right idea, even though it wasn't accompanied by a great attitude. Dessert is the great political equalizer, loved by rich and poor, meek and powerful alike. And Bill is not exempt, being the quintessential man of the people. But then neither was the father of our country, who spent $200 one summer on ice cream.

CHELSEA'S BIRTHDAY CARROT CAKE

Almost every year on her birthday, Chelsea Clinton requests a carrot cake. Said to be a quick study at school, Bill's only child apparently learned early on that if she wanted to have her cake and get to eat it, too, she'd better choose a recipe that wasn't also Dad's favorite. Bill's birthday request? Chelsea would tell you to bet on Sweet-Tooth's Sweet Potato Pie (page 102).

1 ¼ cups vegetable oil
2 cups sugar
4 eggs
2 cups all-purpose flour
2 teaspoons baking powder
1 teaspoon soda
1 teaspoon cinnamon
¾ cup ground carrots
½ cup chopped walnuts
½ cup currants
½ cup golden raisins

FOR THE FROSTING:
1 pound soft cream cheese
1 stick butter
2 cups powdered sugar
2 teaspoons vanilla extract

Preheat oven to 350 degrees. Combine oil and sugar, beat well for 3 minutes and add eggs. Add dry ingredients and mix. Add carrots, walnuts, currants and raisins and mix.

Grease and flour pans; pour in cake batter.

Bake for 25 to 30 minutes.

To make the frosting, cream butter and cream cheese well. Add sifted powdered sugar. Add vanilla. Beat 5 minutes. Allow cake to cool before frosting.

FAT CONTENT RATING:

> "He was a great apple-cobbler eater. We would just leave it out on the counter after dinner at night. And it might be there when we came back in the morning and it might not."
>
> —LIZA ASHLEY, former chef, the Arkansas Governor's Mansion

THE OFFICIAL POSITIONS

Washington has never been short on either advice or rules, even when it comes to food. Back in 1887, White House steward Hugo Ziemann and a Mrs. F. L. Gillette compiled the most helpful *White House Cookbook*, "a comprehensive cyclopedia of information for the home, containing cooking, toilet and household recipes, menus, dinner-giving, table etiquette, care of the sick, health suggestions, facts worth knowing, etc." Here are some tidbits of timeless advice on tippling and table manners from the book:

Szathmary Family Culinary Collection JWU

SMALL POINTS ON ETIQUETTE
The stout woman…should shun champagne. She should hate ice cream.

SOUP EATING
Soup is always served for the first course, and it should be eaten with dessert spoons and taken from the sides, not the tips of them, without any sound of the lips and not sucked into the mouth audibly from the end of the spoon.

DINNER GIVING
Each dish should be garnished sufficiently to be in good taste without looking absurd.

MEATS AND THEIR ACCOMPANIMENTS
Lemon juice makes a very graceful addition to nearly all the insipid members of the fish kingdom.

BAKING BREAD
There is no one article of food that enters so largely into our daily fare as bread, so no degree of skill in preparing other articles can compensate for lack of knowledge in the act of making good, palatable and nutritious bread.

HINTS IN REGARD TO HEALTH
A cupful of strong coffee will remove the odor of onions from the breath.

LAST BUT NOT LEAST...
Watercress will neutralize chalk in the blood, which limy matter is the great cause of aging and stiffening of the fibers. Those who would feel young and look young, therefore, should eat watercress.

"I came to Vermont determined to get my cholesterol down—with low-fat Ben & Jerry's Cherry Garcia."

–BILL

WHO SAYS HE HAS NO RESTRAINT?

During the budget deadlock with Congress that led to repeated temporary shutdowns of non-essential government services, Clinton made the ultimate sacrifice—a temporary suspension of sweets. He announced at a dinner, "Secretary Rubin has asked that we all refrain from dessert because the Treasury Department is holding a bake sale in the lobby."

HILLARY'S SEMISWEET REVENGE

She gave up hair bands, a law partnership and even her last name, but Hillary has to draw the line somewhere. "One of the serious issues of our marriage is that Bill Clinton does not eat chocolate," she once said. Of course Bill is allergic, but as with many of his allergies that doesn't mean he never touches the stuff. One can imagine Hil getting through a rough patch by accidentally leaving a batch of these on the counter at night.

This recipe was originally created for *Good Housekeeping* as part of a First Lady cookie bake-off. Barbara Bush's cookies won top honors—and now she's got plenty of time to bake them. Makes 7½ dozen.

1½ cups unsifted all-purpose flour
1½ teaspoon salt
1 teaspoon baking soda
1 cup solid vegetable shortening
1 cup firmly packed light brown sugar
½ cup granulated sugar
1 teaspoon vanilla extract
2 eggs
2 cups old-fashioned rolled oats
1 package (12 ounces) semisweet chocolate chips

Preheat oven to 350 degrees. Spray baking sheets with nonstick cooking spray.

Combine flour, salt and baking soda in large bowl.

Beat together shortening, sugars and vanilla in large bowl with an electric mixer until creamy. Add eggs, beating until light and fluffy. Gradually beat in flour mixture and rolled oats. Stir in chocolate chips.

Drop batter by well-rounded measuring teaspoonfuls onto greased baking sheets.

Bake in oven 8 to 10 minutes or until golden.

Cool cookies by placing sheets on top of a wire rack for 2 minutes. Then place cookies directly on wire rack to cool completely.

FAT CONTENT RATING:

ELI'S CARAMEL PRALINE CHEESECAKE

Marc Schulman, owner of Eli's Finest Cheesecake, likes to brag that his famous cheesecakes put Bill in office. "In March of the election year, a week before the primary, Clinton's chances of getting elected were slim and none," said Schulman. "The fact is that at one o'clock on a Wednesday I got a call informing me that the Governor and Mrs. Clinton would like to come to the bakery to see the people involved in our on-site education program.

"And the fact is this was his last appearance in Illinois before the primary. People involved in Illinois politics talk about this visit as being one of the most significant turning points in the election." Clinton went on to take the pivotal Illinois primary—so who knows what else these cheesecakes can do.

1 9-inch Eli's or other frozen plain cheesecake
½ cup prepared caramel, melted

FOR THE PRALINE TOPPING:
1½ cups all-purpose flour
1 cup brown sugar
8 ounces pecan halves
4 ounces unsalted butter, cut into 1-inch cubes

Preheat oven to 325 degrees. Combine flour, sugar and pecans in mixer bowl and blend until incorporated; add butter and blend into sugar mixture until butter is dispersed and mixture looks very coarse.

Spread mixture on large baking sheet. Bake, stirring occasionally, until mixture turns medium brown. Cool to room temperature, then break into large irregular pieces, about ⅓ to ½ inches.

Spread caramel on top and sides of plain cheesecake; immediately press praline topping over top and side of the cheesecake.

Serve with more caramel sauce, if desired.

FAT CONTENT RATING: 🐘 🐘 🐘 🐘 🐘

HOW TO BECOME A PRESIDENT

On May 8, 1952, young Richard Nixon gave a speech at a New York fundraising dinner. Something about him captured the imagination of his audience, which listened intently and rose for a standing ovation when Nixon finished talking. At the end of the evening, Governor Thomas Dewey shook his hand, saying, "That was a terrific speech. Make me a promise: Don't get fat, don't lose your zeal, and you can be president some day."

BUBBA'S BLUEBERRY PEACH CRISP

Each time the President leaves Martha's Vineyard at the end of a summer visit, a press party is thrown. Our chef, V. Jaime Hamlin Schilcher, catered the last event, in the summer of '94, and she made this crisp especially for Bill. Boy, did he appreciate it! In fact, Bill ate the entire crisp before it even made it to his table. He was leaving the press bash early to make it to a dinner in his honor at the nearby Lambert's Cove Inn and on his way out, peeked into the tent where Jaime was preparing food. "Mr. President," said Jaime, "We have to stop meeting this way." Bill chuckled and proceeded to devour an entire plate of Blueberry Peach Crisp. "And I have to stop eating this way," he said.

4 cups fresh blueberries
2 cups sliced fresh peaches
⅔ cup orange juice
½ cup brown sugar

FOR THE COBBLER TOPPING:
1 cup all-purpose flour
½ teaspoon baking powder
⅛ teaspoon salt
½ pound softened butter
¾ cup sugar
1 egg
½ teaspoon vanilla extract

Preheat oven to 375 degrees. In a large bowl mix fruit with orange juice and brown sugar. In a smaller bowl mix flour, baking powder and salt.

Put into glass 9x13-inch baking dish.

Cream butter and sugar in a large bowl; add egg and vanilla.

Add flour mixture gradually. Dough will be very soft and sticky; drop this by tablespoonfuls onto the fruit mixture.

Bake 30 to 40 minutes or until cobbler topping is brown and bubbly.

FAT CONTENT RATING:

SWEET-TOOTH'S SWEET POTATO PIE

Bill's enduring affection for this low-calorie, fat-free root vegetable (he's adored sweet potatoes since childhood—see Virginia's Sweet Potato, page 78) might be his dietary saving grace if he liked his potato plain, but the President's preference is for sweetened sweet spuds. At least the sweet potato is a good source of vitamin A and it's also guaranteed to be grown in the good old U.S.A., not to be confused with the yam, which is grown in the tropics and tastes starchier and more bitter.

FOR THE PIE CRUST:
2½ cups all-purpose flour
1 cup (2 sticks) butter, cut into small pieces
1 teaspoon salt
1 teaspoon sugar
½ cup ice water
(Makes 2 crusts)

FOR THE FILLING:
4 medium sweet potatoes or yams (peeled and boiled until soft)
3 eggs, beaten
⅓ cup granulated sugar
½ cup brown sugar
½ teaspoon nutmeg
¾ teaspoon cinnamon
½ teaspoon salt
¼ cup candied ginger
1½ cups heavy cream

FOR THE PIE CRUST:

Put flour, butter, salt and sugar in bowl or food processor; process until mixture resembles coarse meal. Add ice water slowly until dough just holds together. Wrap dough in plastic and chill one hour. Divide in half.

Spray pie tin with nonstick cooking spray, roll out chilled dough on floured board, fit into pie tin, crimp edges.

FOR THE FILLING:

Preheat oven to 400 degrees.

Mash sweet potatoes. In a large bowl, combine remaining ingredients. Add sweet potatoes; stir until well mixed. Pour into unbaked pie shell, bake for 45 minutes or until set.

Serve with whipped cream or vanilla ice cream.

FAT CONTENT RATING: 🐘 🐘 🐘

LAISSEZ-FAIRE LEMON CHESS PIE

This populist pie comes from the hostess with the mostest, former Arkansas Governor's Mansion chef, Liza Ashley. Ashley swears that Lemon Chess is Bill's absolute favorite dessert and he likes it topped only with whipped cream, not meringue. We dubbed it Laissez-Faire, which is the French equivalent of "hands off"—a warning frequently voiced by Liza when Bill got up to his mischievous ways and tried to cut himself a piece of her Lemon Chess before it had cooled properly.

2 cups sugar
½ cup butter or margarine
5 eggs
1 cup milk
1 tablespoon all-purpose flour
1 tablespoon cornmeal
¼ cup fresh lemon juice
Rind of 3 lemons grated
1 9-inch unbaked pie shell

Preheat oven to 350 degrees. Cream sugar and butter; add eggs and milk. Beat well. Add flour, cornmeal, lemon juice and lemon rind.

Pour mixture into pie shell; bake until done, 35 to 45 minutes.

FAT CONTENT RATING:

On the night of his second inauguration, President Lincoln and his wife greeted guests at the White House for four hours, as the 15,000 well-wishers filed through the receiving line that Saturday evening. On Monday the Inaugural Ball gave the First Lady another rare opportunity for dressing up. She wore a $2,000 dress of white silk and lace to the ball.

BILL OF FARE
OF THE
Presidential Inauguration Ball
IN THE
CITY OF WASHINGTON, D. C.,
On the 6th of March 1865.

Oyster Stews ....
Terrapin " ....
Oysters, pickled ....

BEEF.
Roast Beef ....
Filet de Beef ....
Beef à-la-mode ....
Beef à l'anglais ....

VEAL.
Leg of Veal ....
Fricandeau ....
Veal Malakoff ....

POULTRY.
Roast Turkey ....
Boned " ....
Roast Chicken ....
Grouse, boned and roast .....

GAME.
Pheasant ....
Quail ....
Venison ....

PATETES.
Patète of Duck en gelée ......
Patète de fois gras ....

SMOKED.
Ham ....
Tongue en gelée ....
do   plain ....

SALADES.
Chicken ....
Lobster ....

Ornamental Pyramides.
Nougate ....
Orange ....
Caramel with Fancy Cream Candy
Coconaut ....
Macaroon ....

Croquant ....
Chocolate ....
Tres Cakes ....

CAKES AND TARTS.
Almond Sponge ....
Belle Alliance ....
Dame Blanche ....
Macaroon Tart ....
Tart à la Nelson ....
Tarte à l'Orleans ....
do   à la Portugaise ....
do   à la Vienne ....
Pound Cake ....
Sponge Cake ....
Lady Cake ....
Fancy small Cakes ....

JELLIES AND CREAMS.
Calfsfoot and Wine Jelly ......
Charlotte à la Russe ....
do   do Vanilla ....
Blanc Mangue ....
Crème Neapolitane ....
do   à la Nelson ....
do   Chateaubriand ....
do   à la Smyrna ....
do   do Nesselrode ......
Bombe à la Vanilla ....

ICE CREAM.
Vanilla ....
Lemon ....
White Coffee ....
Chocolate ....
Burnt Almonds ....
Maraschino ....

FRUIT ICES.
Strawberry ....
Orange ....
Lemon ....

DESSERT.
Grapes, Almonds, Raisins, &c.
Coffee and Chocolate.

Furnished by **G. A. BALZER**, CONFECTIONER,
Cor. 9th & D Sts., Washington, D. C.

Szathmary Family Culinary Collection JWU

MELLO JELL-O PINEAPPLE 7-UP SALAD

This one comes from Liza Ashley, the former chef at the Arkansas Governor's Mansion who gave us Slick Willie's Wishbone Tenders (page 25), Liza's Hot Chicken Salad (page 47) and Laissez-Faire Lemon Chess Pie (page 104). With the exception of Hillary, Liza knows more than anyone about what foods make Bill happy and relaxed, and this is certainly the dessert to feed him on a balmy summer evening when the day's work is done.

1 3-ounce package lime Jell-O
1 15-ounce can crushed pineapple
8 ounces cream cheese
1 10-ounce bottle 7-Up
2 cups chopped nuts

Place Jello mix, pineapple and cream cheese in saucepan over low heat; heat until Jello dissolves, stirring constantly. Remove from heat and add 7-Up. Add chopped nuts. Pour into mold.

Chill 3 hours or overnight.

FAT CONTENT RATING: 🐘 🐘 🐘

PUDDING CAKE DESSERT

How can anything made with a whole container of Cool Whip, a pint of raspberries and chocolate be bad? This is the ultimate combination of food America loves. Add a few blueberries and serve it on the Fourth of July!

½ cup (1 stick) butter
¼ cup sugar
1 cup all-purpose flour
1 cup chopped pecans
8 ounces cream cheese
¾ cup plus 2 tablespoons confectioner's sugar
1 large container Cool Whip
1 4½-ounce package instant chocolate pudding
1 ¾-ounce package instant French vanilla pudding (add ½ tablespoon
    vanilla extract and 2 tablespoons confectioner's sugar)
4 cups cold milk
Grated chocolate
1 pint fresh raspberries

Preheat oven to 350 degrees. In a medium bowl combine softened butter, sugar, flour and pecans. Press into 13x9x2-inch pan and bake for 20 minutes. Set aside on a rack to cool.

Blend cream cheese, confectioner's sugar and 1 cup of the Cool Whip. Spread over cooled crust.

Blend instant puddings with milk until thick. Spread over cream cheese filling. Top with remaining Cool Whip.

Grate chocolate over top if desired. Chill well. Garnish with raspberries.

FAT CONTENT RATING:

"They have wonderful cooks here. As Chelsea could tell you, there is a whole little kitchen where they don't do anything but make pastry and sweet things."

—BILL,
addressing children in
a TV special

Secret Service

Many people think that good cooking is all about secret techniques and tricks. But you will find that if you use quality ingredients and follow the directions, cooking can be a snap. Of course you need to remember our simple Clinton rule: Never put anything in the oven that contains a plastic cooking implement. The following pages include hints on making your food fatty and tasty enough to tempt a president, as well as tips on stocking a pantry Clinton-style.

JAIME'S HIGH-FAT COOKING TECHNIQUES

If anyone could make me appreciate the pleasure of high-fat flavors, it would be Bill. The first time I met him, I felt as if he threw blue sparks—he's a very charismatic man with a glimmer in his eye. He's also the consummate politician, a true populist who genuinely believes that he and Hillary can make a difference.

That first meeting was at the Martha's Vineyard airport, where my sons and I were waiting on the runway as Air Force One landed. We were invited to meet Bill as I would be cooking that evening for his 47th birthday party. As the President shook my hand, his good friend and mine, Vernon Jordan, said, "This is the woman who's going to be cooking your dinner." Bill smiled and said, "Well, you better get going."

Everybody knows that what gives food its flavor is fat. I find that if you use copious quantities of butter and heavy cream everything you make will taste better. Lots of gooey cheese melted over just about anything is delicious too! Smooth-melt cheese is a generic name for brands like Velveeta that blend actual cheese with other ingredients to make it melt in a smooth-and-creamy layer on top of hamburgers, eggs or cauliflower.

If you've had a typical American breakfast of bacon and eggs, hang on to that bacon grease. It adds great flavor to hash browns, or can be used to sauté onions and garlic in for dinner. Bacon fat is also an ideal medium for making roux, a flour and fat mixture that is used to thicken sauces (see Charity Chicken and Sausage Gumbo, page 52, or Pentagon Stuffed Pork Chops, page 30). If you add some chicken stock and heavy cream to the roux you have a great sauce for pork chops or Chin-Up Chicken Fried Steak (page 24)—"Stuff-stuff with heavy," as writer Calvin Trillin would say. My friend Margot's grandmother used to rub bacon grease on the skins of baked potatoes to make them extra crispy.

Never take the skin off chicken or turkey. That's where all the flavor is.

If you must steam something (broccoli, for instance) melt some butter and sauté it for a few minutes before serving.

Whole milk and full fat sour cream are much better tasting than the 1% or "fat-free" varieties. Many people think that margarine is better for you than butter. Wrong. They both have about 100 calories and 14 grams fat per tablespoon and butter tastes so much better.

Feel free to slather regular (never the fat-free kind!) mayonnaise on sandwiches to moisten them. We've jazzed it up with scallions or hot jalapeño peppers in some of the recipes.

Several tablespoons of olive or vegetable oil brought to a high temperature are ideal for sautéing vegetables (see Hillary's Beijing Stir-Fry, page 84). Be sure vegetables are free of excess moisture as the oil will splatter if they're put in the oil wet.

They say fat is the favorite American food group and is a far more popular nutrient than protein in the American diet. Studies show that the average person consumes the equivalent of one stick of butter a day.

–V. JAIME HAMLIN SCHILCHER

ABOUT THE CHEF

V. Jaime Hamlin Schilcher is a Democrat and a big supporter of Bill's who has been catering on Martha's Vineyard for 20 years. She is the owner of V. Jaime Hamlin Catering and Party Design, a company specializing in weddings. Her client list includes Ambassador Henry Grunwald, Mike Wallace, William Styron, Ted Danson, Mary Steenburgen and of course Bill Clinton whenever he's on the island and a special occasion calls for a celebratory feast. Schilcher and former husband Raymond Schilcher catered the President's birthday and collaborated on *The Oyster Bar Cookbook* (Rizzoli), a collection of recipes from their Oyster Bar Restaurant in New York City. She has prepared food in London, Paris and New York and is the mother of four boys. She created the food design for the Martha's Vineyard scenes of the Harrison Ford–Julia Ormond movie, *Sabrina*.

MAIL-ORDER SOURCES

Balducci's
11-02 Queens Plaza South
Long Island City, NY 11101-4908
(800) 225-3822
Fresh pastas, sauces, prime meats, desserts

Bundon Foods, Inc.
Box 1668
Bandon, OR 97411
(503) 347-2456 or (800) 548-8961
Hand-Cheddared, full-cream white Cheddar

Gates Bar-B-Q
4707 Paseo
Kansas City, MO 64110
(816) 923-0900
*Seasonings and barbecue sauce in the following flavors: Original Classic,
Extra Hot, Sweet and Mild, Mild, Natural*

Jane Butel's Pecos Valley Spice Co.
4371 Charlotte Highway
3 Heritage Park
Lake Wylie, SC 29710
(803) 831-0121
Spices and seasonings

Dole's Exotic Game Meats
214 Denargo Market
Denver, CO 80216
(303) 297-WILD
Buffalo cuts, venison, elk, wild boar, duck, pheasant, wild turkey; exotics like alligator, rattlesnake, snapping turtle.

Ozark Mountain Family Smokehouse
P.O. Box 37
Farmington, AR 72730-0037
(501) 267-3567
Arkansas bacon, assorted bacons and meats, preserves

Texas Wild Game Cooperative
P.O. Box 530
Ingram, TX 78025
(800) 962-4263
Prime supplier of Texas axis venison, black buck antelope, wild boar, smoked sausages

PANTRY STOCKING TIPS

With the following ingredients in hand, you can make just every recipe in this book.

FLOUR AND BAKING
  RELATED ITEMS

White flour
All-purpose flour, unbleached
Rolled oats, old-fashioned
Prepared pie crusts
  (keep frozen)
Brown sugar
Baking powder
Baking soda
Dry yeast packets
Yellow cornmeal
Masa Harina
  (very fine, treated cornmeal)
Confectioner's Sugar
Instant vanilla pudding
Instant chocolate pudding

OILS

Vegetable or corn oil
Vegetable oil cooking spray
Butter
Margarine
Good-quality olive oil
  (Spanish olive oil has more
  flavor and is usually less
  expensive than Italian or
  French olive oil)
Italian salad dressing
  (great for marinating)
Sesame oil

SEASONINGS (WET)

Fresh garlic
Fresh green or red chili peppers
Horseradish (bottled)
Mayonnaise
Molasses
Mustard
    (Dijon and yellow
    "ballpark" type)
Soy sauce
Tabasco
Tomato paste
Vinegar
    (apple cider and balsamic)
Worcestershire sauce

OTHER BASICS

Canned beef broth
Canned black pitted olives
Canned chicken broth
Cheese
    (American, Cheddar, Monterey
    Jack, smooth-melt)
Cream cheese
Crushed pineapple
Cool Whip
Flour tortillas
Canned green chilies
    (mild or hot)
Heavy cream
Lime Jell-O
Maple syrup
Mini-marshmallows
Nacho-flavored corn chips
Nuts (pecans or walnuts)
Onions
Raisins (golden and regular)
Ranch dressing
Red kidney beans (canned)
Refried beans
Salsa
Scallions
Sour cream
Canned tomatoes
    (whole and crushed)
Tuna (oil- or water-packed)

ABOUT THE AUTHOR

Anonymous is well-known around the country as a bestselling author. The publisher remains unaware of the author's true identity, having only communicated via e-mail during the writing and editing of this book. The author is currently using the screen name "Deep Fat."

"Well, everything."

–HILLARY CLINTON,
on what food President Clinton likes best.